SCHUMANN

Books by David Whitwell

Philosophic Foundations of Education
Foundations of Music Education
Music Education of the Future
The Sousa Oral History Project
The Art of Musical Conducting
The Longy Club: 1900–1917
A Concise History of the Wind Band
Wagner on Bands
Berlioz on Bands
Chopin: A Self-Portrait
La Téléphonie and the Universal Musical Language
Extraordinary Women
Aesthetics of Music in Ancient Civilizations
Aesthetics of Music in the Middle Ages
Aesthetics of Music in the Early Renaissance

The History and Literature of the Wind Band and Wind Ensemble Series

Volume 1 The Wind Band and Wind Ensemble Before 1500
Volume 2 The Renaissance Wind Band and Wind Ensemble
Volume 3 The Baroque Wind Band and Wind Ensemble
Volume 4 The Wind Band and Wind Ensemble of the Classical Period (1750–1800)
Volume 5 The Nineteenth-Century Wind Band and Wind Ensemble
Volume 6 A Catalog of Multi-Part Repertoire for Wind Instruments or for Undesignated Instrumentation before 1600
Volume 7 Baroque Wind Band and Wind Ensemble Repertoire
Volume 8 Classical Period Wind Band and Wind Ensemble Repertoire
Volume 9 Nineteenth-Century Wind Band and Wind Ensemble Repertoire
Volume 10 A Supplementary Catalog of Wind Band and Wind Ensemble Repertoire
Volume 11 A Catalog of Wind Repertoire before the Twentieth Century for One to Five Players
Volume 12 A Second Supplementary Catalog of Early Wind Band and Wind Ensemble Repertoire
Volume 13 Name Index, Volumes 1–12, The History and Literature of the Wind Band and Wind Ensemble

www.whitwellbooks.com

SCHUMANN: A SELF-PORTRAIT IN HIS OWN WORDS

David Whitwell

Whitwell Publishing: Austin, Texas, USA

Schumann: A Self-Portrait In His Own Words
Second Edition
Dr. David Whitwell

WHITWELL PUBLISHING
815-A BRAZOS ST. #491
AUSTIN, TX 78701
WWW.WHITWELLPUBLISHING.COM

© 1986, 2012 by David Whitwell
All rights reserved. First edition 1986.
Second edition 2012

Composed in Bembo Book.
Published in the United States of America.
All images used in this book are in the public domain except where otherwise noted.

ISBN-13: 978-1-936512-47-8
ISBN-10: 1936512475

Contents

Primary Sources vii

Acknowledgment vii

Foreword viii

A Brief Chronology of the Life of Robert Schumann x

Part I: Schumann's Reflections on his own Music

Chapter One: Schumann on His Own Musical Studies 3

Chapter Two: Schumann's General Outlook on Music 5

Chapter Three: Schumann on The Public and Posterity 17

Chapter Four: Schumann on His Own Creative Process 21

Chapter Five: Schumann on His Own Compositions 29

Part II Schumann's View of the World of Music

Chapter Six: Schumann on Criticism 39

Chapter Seven: Schumann on Performance 41

Chapter Eight: Schumann on Music Education 47

    Suggestions for Young Composers 47

    On Teaching 51

    Maxims for Young Musicians 53

Chapter Nine: Of Foreign Lands and Peoples 61

    Italy 61

    France 61

Germany	62
Bohemia	62
Vienna	62
Bach	65
Beethoven	67
Berlioz	68
Brahms	70
Cherubini	71
Chopin	71
Czerny	74
Dreyschack	75
Handel	75
Lachner	75
Liszt	76
Mendelssohn	79
Meyerbeer	83
Mozart	84
Rossini	85
Schubert	85
Thalberg	88
Wagner	88
Weber	89

Part III Schumann: A Self-Portrait

Chapter Ten: Schumann on His Personality and Character Traits 93

Chapter Eleven: Schumann on His Health and Mental Attitude 103

Chapter Twelve: Insights into Schumann's General Outlook on Life 113

    Living 113

    Time And Aging 114

    Faith 115

    Friends 117

    Nature 118

    Love 118

    Women 119

    Arts 120

Chapter Thirteen: Schumann's Reflections on His Life as a Student 123

Chapter Fourteen: Schumann's Reflections on His Daily Routine 131

Chapter Fifteen: Schumann's Descriptions of His Wife, Clara 135

Chapter Fifteen: On the Founding of the *Neue Zeitschrift Für Musik* 141

PRIMARY SOURCES

May Herbert (trans.), *Early Letters of Robert Schumann*. London: Bell and Sons, 1888.

Fanny Raymond Ritter (trans.), *Music and Musicians*, two volumes of translations from the *Neue Zeitschrift für Musik*. London: W. Reeves, 1877, 1880.

Karl Storck (ed.), *The Letters of Robert Schumann*. London, 1907.

ACKNOWLEDGEMENT

We wish to acknowledge our gratitude to the professional graphic artist, Daniel Ferla, for his important help in making possible this new edition of a work first published in 1986.

FOREWORD

This volume is not intended to be the traditional kind of autobiography, which all too often relegates the reader to the role of one on the side-line who can only observe the procession of dates, people, and facts which define the life of the subject. The purpose of the present volume is quite different. Here we will pass by the usual parade of events and happenings of Schumann's life (excepting the brief chronological sketch below) and concentrate instead on his own thoughts, as expressed in his own words.

The purpose has been to bring together Schumann's thoughts, drawn from many years and a variety of sources, and to present his thoughts chronologically by subject, to permit the reader insights into Schumann's thinking on a subject and the development of these thoughts as they surface during his lifetime.

Apart from selecting subjects which would be of interest to the modern reader, the actual selection of the material herein has been limited to only those comments by Schumann which seem to offer revelation on the man and his music. For example, not every reference to a particular composition has been included, but rather only those which might offer the reader an insight into how Schumann himself viewed that composition.

With the hope of allowing the reader the most direct possible relationship with this master composer, I have resisted the strong and constant urge to add connecting or amplifying text and have left Schumann's own thoughts to speak for themselves. My own experience in reading this material has been that I have felt a much closer relationship with Schumann the man, something I somehow never quite achieved from traditional accounts of this master and his music. It is my hope that perhaps the reader as well might enjoy this experience.

David Whitwell
Austin, Texas

A BRIEF CHRONOLOGY OF THE LIFE OF ROBERT SCHUMANN

Robert Schumann was born in 1810 in Zwickau, in Saxony, now East Germany. As a young boy, Schumann displayed talent both in his music and literary efforts, but his father, a businessman, determined that Robert should study law. His days as a university law student in Leipzig and Heidelberg were characterized both by participation in student life of the time and a continuing struggle to determine the course of his future.

His romantic interest in Clara Wieck, daughter to one of his teachers, also dates from 1835 and begins a long period of suffering in his attempts to win her hand from the protective, and even hostile, father. A number of important compositions for piano and the acquisition of an honorary doctorate contributed to his standing, but it was through legal action that his marriage with Clara was made possible.

In 1844 Schumann established residence in Dresden, and this period saw very prolific composition in all forms. He met with less success, however, in his long desire to obtain an official position which would offer him public recognition and economic stability. In 1850 he accepted such a position in Düsseldorf, but by this time his physical and mental health had deteriorated significantly and in his stay in Düsseldorf he largely failed in both his personal and artistic relationships.

His mental condition, symptoms of which can be traced over most of his adult life, turned rapidly for the worse in February, 1854, and in March he was taken to an asylum, where he died in the summer of 1856.

Part I

Schumann's Reflections On His Own Music

Chapter One

Schumann on his own Musical Studies

1828

I am very often with Wieck, who teaches me the piano, and there I get the chance every day of making the acquaintance of the most excellent musicians in Leipzig.[1]

1. Letter to his Mother, Leipzig, August 22, 1828.

1830

I shall go to Weimar to be under Hummel, for the deep reason that I may *call myself* a pupil of his.[2]

2. Letter to his Mother, Leipzig, December 12, 1830.

1831

To give you an idea of the vigorous reforms my teacher had to institute, I must tell you that, although I could play any concerto at sight, I had to go back and learn the scale of C major. I returned to Leipzig fired with enthusiasm and armed with the firmest resolves. But what a change did I find in my old master! Contrary to his former method of weighing each note critically and studying each movement conscientiously page by page, he let me scramble through good and bad alike, neglecting both touch and fingering. His one idea was to secure a brilliant, pseudo-Paganini performance, and I could hardly play splashily enough to please him. My master wished to rid me of a certain cautious, mechanical and studied manner of playing.[3]

3. Letter to Johann Nepomuk Hummel, Leipzig, August 20, 1831.

1832

I now see the inestimable value of theoretical studies; it is only the abuse of them which is harmful.[4]

4. Letter to Heinrich Dorn, Leipzig, April 25, 1832.

My theoretical studies with Dorn have been of great value in bringing my mind, through steady application, to a state of clearness, before which I have often dimly striven.[5]

5. Letter to his Mother, Leipzig, May 8, 1832.

A few months ago I finished my theoretical course with Dorn, having got as far as canons, which I have been studying by myself after Marpurg, who is a capital theorist. Otherwise Sebastian Bach's *Wohltemperirtes Clavier* is my grammar, and it is certainly the best. I have taken the fugues one by one, and dissected them down to their minutest parts. The advantage of this is great, and seems to have a strengthening moral effect upon one's whole system; for Bach was a thorough man, all over. There is nothing sickly or stunted about him, and his works seem written for eternity. Now I must learn to read scores and study instrumentation.[6]

6. Letter to Baccalaureus Kuntzsch, Leipzig, July 27, 1832.

1838

Bach is my daily bread; he comforts me and gives me new ideas. I think it was Beethoven who said, 'Compared to him we are all children.'[7]

7. Letter to Clara Wieck, Leipzig, March, 1838. The Beethoven reference was actually to Handel.

I give several hours daily to the serious study of Bach and Beethoven, outside my own studies.[8]

8. Letter to Clara Wieck, Leipzig, May 10, 1838.

1839

You know our great author Jean Paul? I have learnt more counterpoint from him than from my music teacher.[9]

9. Letter to Simonin de Sire, Vienna, March 15, 1839.

1851

My compositions—the larger works especially—might, I imagine, convince you of my acquaintance with the great masters. It is *to them* I go, and have always gone, for advice. To Gluck, the simple; to Handel, the complicated and to Bach the most complicated of all. Let me recommend to you to the study of Bach, my most complicated works will thereafter seem simple enough.[10]

10. Letter to J. N., Düsseldorf, September 22, 1851.

Chapter Two

Schumann's General Outlook on Music

1832

I soon decided that just as excess or misuse of the finest and noblest things produces satiety and indifference, so does intelligent, conscientious, preserving work alone secure progress, and preserve the charm in any art, especially in music. The stronger the original impulse, the greater is the reaction.[1]

Music is to me the perfect expression of the soul, while to some it is a mere intoxication of the sense of hearing, and to others an arithmetical problem and treated as such.[2]

1833

The artist should be cheerful as a Grecian god, in his intercourse with life and men. But when these dare to approach too near, he should disappear, leaving nothing but clouds behind him.

. . . . . .

The artist should preserve his equilibrium with life, or else his position becomes difficult.

. . . . . .

It is the curse of talent that, although it labors more steadily and perseveringly than genius, it does not reach a goal. Genius, floating on the summit of the ideal, gazes from above, serenely smiling.

. . . . . .

Genius. We forgive the diamond its sharp edges. It is costly labor to round them.

. . . . . .

---

1. Letter to his Mother, Leipzig, May 8, 1832.

2. Letter to his Mother, Leipzig, August 9, 1832.

The misfortune of the imitator is, that he can only appropriate the salient points of his original. An involuntary awe disables him from copying its peculiar beauties.

......

It is not a good thing to have acquired too much facility in any occupation.

......

We were at the goal? We err. Art is a great fugue, into which different individualities and nationalities step and become resolved, like the different subjects, one after another.

......

He who sets limits for himself, will always be expected to remain within them.

......

They should remember that the seventh once displeased as much as the diminished octave does now. It is through harmonic development that music has attained such a high rank among the arts and has acquired the power of expressing the finest shades of passion and the deepest feelings of the soul.

......

The 'triad epoch.' For the third, like the present, is the mediation between past and future.

......

The youthful works of masters who have become great, are looked upon with very different eyes than are the works of composers who promised as much, but did not keep their word.

......

Dare talent permit itself to take the same liberties as genius?

......

The emptiest head thinks it can hide its weakness behind a fugue, but a true fugue is the affair of a great master.

......

The first conception is always the most natural and the best. The understanding may err, but not the feelings.

......

Ye peddlers in art, do ye not sink into the earth when ye are reminded of the words uttered by Beethoven on his dying bed: 'I believe I am yet but at the beginning?'

......

Talent labors, genius creates.

......

The Great is admirable, even in ruin. Dismember a symphony by Beethoven and one by Gyrowetz, and then observe what remains. Works of mere talent or compilation, when destroyed, seem but overturned card houses; while, after the expiration of centuries, pillars and capitals of ruined temples still exist.

......

Your declaration, Florestan, that you admire the pastoral and heroic symphonies less, because Beethoven has so designated them, and thus set limits to our imagination, seems to me to be founded on a just feeling. But if you ask me why, I scarcely know how to answer.

......

He who is anxious to preserve his originality, is in danger of losing it.

......

Few strikingly original works of genius have become popular.

......

I have sometimes thought that the style in which composers illustrate their works by signs of expression enlightens us sooner as to their aesthetic cultivation than do the very tones they combine.

......

No one does more than he knows. No one knows more than he does.

......

That would be but a small art indeed that merely possessed sounds, but no speech, no symbol fitted to express the varying movements of the soul.

......

Great thoughts often circulate in similar words and tone, through different minds.[3]

1834

Music develops and transforms itself with a rapidity of which no other art offers an example; and it often happens that even the best is only esteemed among contemporaries for the space of a decade. The intolerance of young minds, thanklessly forgetful of this, and unregardful of the fact that they are merely building up a height of which they did not lay the foundation, is an experience that has been, and will be, made in every epoch of art.[4]

1835

Musical, like political, revolutions penetrate under the lowest roof into the smallest matter. In music we observe the new influence in precisely that branch where art is sensuously allied to common life—in the dance. As contrapuntal predominance disappeared, miniature sarabands and gavottes, hoops and patches, went out of fashion, and pigtails became much shorter. Then the minuets of Mozart and Haydn rustled in by their long trains, while people stood facing each other decorously and silently, bowing often, and finally walking away; a grave peruke was still to be seen here and there, but the hitherto stiffy-laced figures already began to move more gracefully and elastically. Then young Beethoven broke in, breathless, yet embarrassed and disturbed, with long, disordered hair, neck and brow free as Hamlet's, and people were greatly astonished at the eccentric fellow; but the ballrooms were too narrow and tiresome for him, so he rushed out into the darkness, through thick and then, elbowing fashion and ceremony, but moving aside lest he should step on the flowers; and those who are pleased with such a nature called it caprice, or anything you like. And then a new generation grew up; the children became youths and maidens, and shy, so dreamy, that they scarcely ventured to look at each other.[5]

Certain half geniuses are to be found, endowed with remarkable liveliness of intellect, united to an unusual receptivity for the extraordinary—whether good or bad—and great facility in appropriating and working it out. One of their

3. Schumann's Diary, 1833 or before.

4. 'From the Criticisms of the Davidsbündler,' *Neue Zeitschrift für Musik*, 1834.

5. 'Short and Rhapsodic Works for Pianoforte,' in *Neue Zeitschrift für Musik*, 1835.

wings is that of genius, the other is plumed with waxen feathers. At a favorable moment, during excitment, one carries the other on high; but, in a normal condition of repose, the waxen wing drags lamely after its fellow.⁶

6. 'New Sonatas for the Piano,' in *Neue Zeitschrift für Musik*, 1835.

1836

It sometimes happens to us artists, when we have spent half a day in study, that we fall among a troop of amateurs, and the most dangerous of all, those who know Beethoven's symphonies.

One begins, 'Sir, true art reached its culminating point in Beethoven. All beyond that is a sin; we must return to the old road.'

Another answers, 'Sir, you do not know young Berlioz. A new era commenced with him; music will again return to the source when it proceeded—to speech itself.'

'It is plain,' proceeds the first, 'that Mendelssohn intended this in his overtures, etc.' One of us sits among them, silent, though inwardly raging (unluckily we musicians can generally do everything better than talk and lay down laws.⁷

7. 'Critical Reviews,' in *Neue Zeitschrift für Musik*, 1836.

Whoever invented the first variations was certainly no bad fellow (and after all, it was Bach again). One cannot write or listen to symphonies every day, and imagination will take refuge in that graceful recreation from which Beethoven's genius has called forth ideal art forms. But the most flourishing period of the variation is approaching its end and making way for the capriccio. May it rest in peace! For no musical form has produced more insipidity than the variation form ... One has little idea how much shameless vulgarity, what poverty, blossoms in these depths. Once we had respectably tiresome German airs, now we have hackneyed Italian ones to swallow in five or six watery decompositions. And we may be thankful to escape with so few ... Let us not waste another word. Into the fire with them all!⁸

8. 'Variations for the Pianoforte,' in *Neue Zeitschrift für Musik*, 1836.

1837

Nature would exhaust herself, if she continually produced Beethovens.⁹

9. 'Chamber Music,' in *Neue Zeitschrift für Musik*, 1837.

We believe Reissiger treats his talent with too much indulgence; greater success should result from so many gifts. I expected his quartet to turn out just what I have found it to be—very entertaining, graceful and melodious, a recreation for artists and not too laborious for amateurs ... We are sure that Reissiger must be able to write a work of deeper contents, one that will resound beyond the limits of the brief present; and such he should produce, unless he means to spoil his players for the study of more difficult and serious things, by common passages that secure speedy applause from the public. But the praise of the stricter critic, whose glance ever seeks the noblest in art, should also be desired and honored; and this would also be granted, were it not for the too visible thirst for applause.[10]

We might often be angry at the caprice displayed by nature in distributing her gifts. To one she gives character, but stiffness, to another invention, but frivolity; one is ambitious, but not preserving; another has poetic thought, but no mechanical talent; many have much, but the most have little.[11]

However desirable it may seem, we cannot all be Bachs at every moment.[12]

1838

Young artists, who always desire something novel, and, if possible, eccentric, esteem too lightly the easily conceived and perfected works of finished masters, and are greatly mistaken in supposing that they could accomplish the same thing equally well. The difference between master and scholar can never be overcome. The hastily thrown off pianoforte sonatas of Beethoven, and still more those of Mozart, are equal proofs in their heavenly ease of these masters' pre-eminence, as are their deeper manifestations.[13]

What can be said of a work that certainly displays preference for noble models, and striving towards an ideal, but that yet produces so little effect, that we envy the talent of Strauss, who shakes melodies out of his sleeves and gold into his pockets. Shall we blame? Shall we mortify a composer who has done all that is possible to him? Shall we praise, where we feel that we have not experienced any real pleasure? ...

10. 'Chamber Music,' in *Neue Zeitschrift für Musik*, 1837.

11. 'Rondos for Pianoforte,' in *Neue Zeitschrift für Musik*, 1837.

12. 'Variations for the Pianoforte,' in *Neue Zeitschrift für Musik*, 1837.

13. 'First Quartet Morning,' in *Neue Zeitschrift für Musik*, 1838.

We prefer to bear witness to the artistic zeal of those who compose without the inspiration of genius, and at the same time advise them not to publish …[14]

The beautiful can only be enjoyed in moderation; and I could more easily spend a night in listening to Strauss and Lanner dance music than to Beethoven symphonies, the tones of which pierce the soul until its wounds ache.[15]

When I have in mind the highest description of music, such as Bach and Beethoven have bestowed on us in some of their creations, when I speak of those rare moods of mind, such as the artist should inspire in us, I demand that each of his works shall lead me a step forward in the spiritual dominion of art and I demand poetic depth and novelty everywhere, in detail as well as in the whole.[16]

When I listened the second time, certain passages already began to annoy me. Passages that sin, not against the first rules of the schools, but against the ear and the natural laws of harmonic progression. I do not count fifths among these only, but also some conclusions in the bass, and some modulations, such as we meet with in inexperienced writers. These faults were as disagreeable to my musicians as to me. There is a sort of instinctive mastery of cadences that seem to be in the gift of nature, upon which that ordinary musical understanding, common to nearly all professional musicians, is grounded. If a young composer offends against this, it matters not how intellectual he may be, he is certain to find such men draw back from him, and scarcely even regard him as one of them. Whence comes this lack of a refined sense of hearing, of a correct management of harmony, amid so many other great gifts? Did the composer discover his talent too late? Did he abandon study too soon? Is it that, in his richness of idea, his command of a generally very deep principal melody, full of meaning, in the upper part, he is unable to invent equally well for the lower ones? or are his organs of hearing really inefficient? This is a great question, as also is that, as to whether or not there is any help for the fault.[17]

14. 'Second Quartet Morning, on the music of C. Decker,' in *Neue Zeitschrift für Musik*, 1838.

15. 'Third Quartet Morning,' in *Neue Zeitschrift für Musik*, 1838.

16. 'Third Quartet Morning,' in *Neue Zeitschrift für Musik*, 1838.

17. 'Fourth and Fifth Quartet Mornings, on the music of Hermann Hirschbach,' in *Neue Zeitschrift für Musik*, 1838.

People compose for many reasons—for the sake of immortality, because the pianoforte happens to be open, to become a millionaire, because friends praise, because one has looked into beautiful eyes, or for no reason at all.[18]

I believe the science of sound, considered as the soul's speech, to be still in its infancy. May my good genius inspire me, and bring me this undeveloped science to maturity.[19]

1839

These sonatas seldom transgress the prosaic boundaries of the quiet study. I see the composer sitting and writing quietly, and secretly reflecting now and then on a nice little immortality. Let him now absorb grander impressions, whether from Bach or Beethoven, from exciting reading or from frequent intercourse with the riches of the universe.[20]

A masterly work cannot be entirely slaughtered even by bunglers.[21]

How endlessly great is the kingdom of form! How much it leads us to expect and to accomplish, for centuries to come! …
I must confess that these etudes [by Kalkbrenner] put me into a melancholy frame of mind. Imagination, where are thou? Ideas, where are ye? I felt inclined to cry out at every page. No answer. Scarcely anything to be found but dry formulas, beginnings, or endings, the picture of an old, once beautiful coquette. But this is the fate of all artists whose art depends on their instrument only. They amuse us so long as they are young and able to give us something new and brilliantly dexterous. In the meanwhile younger talent makes its appearance, and difficulties that once astonished become sport to us all. These artists, accustomed to applause, cannot live without it, and endeavor to force it; but no hand is moved by their efforts, and the multitude smiles where it formerly wondered. Kalkbrenner himself acknowledges that he has devoted a great part of his life to the mechanical cultivation of his hands; this would cause even a Beethovenian composer to deteriorate, putting lesser talent out of the question. And in

18. 'Rondos for the Pianoforte,' in *Neue Zeitschrift für Musik*, 1838.

19. Letter to Simonin de Sire, Leipzig, February 8, 1838.

20. 'On the Music of L. Berger; Sonatas for the Klavier,' in *Neue Zeitschrift für Musik*, 1839.

21. 'Sonatas for Pianoforte,' in *Neue Zeitschrift für Musik*, 1839.

age everything comes to light that the enamel of youth concealed; the lack of profound and varied knowledge, neglect of the study of great preceding models. Could we imagine an unimaginative Sebastian Bach or Beethoven, such a man would still be able to produce interesting works in old age, merely because of his study and acquired science. He who has learned but little may produce graceful things up to a certain age; but then his strength will fail to answer the demands that are made on a man of ripe age; and any unnatural means that may be resorted to, conceal this weakness, will only render it more apparent.[22]

The romantic element does not depend upon figures and forms; it will always appear if the composer is anything of a poet.[23]

1841

If an artist defends himself with the excuse that he ought not to be judged from small pieces, we must answer that the artist should forgive nothing to himself when he has anything to do with publicity. Between our own four walls we may occasionally give way to frivolity, but before the world it is injurious.[24]

He who can read is no longer satisfied in merely spelling. He who understands Shakespeare has got beyond Robinson Crusoe. In short, the sonata style of 1790 is no longer that of 1840; requirements in regard both to form and content have largely increased.[25]

No one ever commenced as a master, and those deeper secrets of our art, that all-powerfully command every heart, are often only to be attained, even by the most talented of its disciples, at a very advanced age.[26]

1842

Life, especially artistic life, is too short to be lived through in butterfly fashion ... The applause of the multitude, the smiles of sentimental women, are poison-flowers to such a nature. The true artist is initiated in a different manner; in solitude, or in the society of other artists, and nothing is so enervating as

22. 'Etudes for the Pianoforte,' in *Neue Zeitschrift für Musik*, 1839.

23. Letter to Clara Wieck, Vienna, January 24, 1839.

24. 'Short Studies for Pianforte,' in *Neue Zeitschrift für Musik*, 1841

25. 'New Sonatas for the Pianoforte,' in *Neue Zeitschrift für Musik*, 1841

26. 'Short Studies for Pianoforte,' in *Neue Zeitschrift für Musik*, 1841.

the favor of mediocrity. No one, it is true, can be more profound than he really is, but everyone can learn and strive …

Every artist's life has its holiday time, when it pleasantly rocks on the waves of the present. But when beckoned to new labors, the hushed voice is no longer silent. The Germans have so many models of lofty manhood. Let our youths look up to these sometimes and to Bach, who considered all works written by himself before his thirtieth year as non-existent. And to Beethoven, who, in his last years, could not bear to hear his own 'Christ on the Mount of Olives.' Do you not tremble, young artists, when you reflect what your opinion regarding your own compositions may be, after fifty? …

The same thing has been said, with the same result, of a hundred other Viennese composers. They want one thing, yet cannot give up the other. The must be artists, and yet please the crowd. Boundless failures in this endeavor have not yet opened their eyes to the fact that nothing can be attained on such a path. Only one path leads to an artistic end and to reach that we must fulfill our duty to ourselves and to art.[27]

Away with passages of thirds and sixths … his is bad Classicism, the pigtail style …
Only a very few of the greatest intellects have accomplished a masterpiece in their opus 4.[28]

Art, to be sure, is no inheritance, its crowns must be earned. Ere the laurel is firmly placed on any poet's head a thousand hands are ready to tear it off, and not with the best intentions. Artistic contests are therefore good to bring out talent more speedily, and to introduce it favorably to the world.[29]

Instruments too often seduce us into mere experimenting, but the voice leads us back to nature.[30]

[Regarding Programmatic titles] No one denies that our art can express much, even the progress of an event. But those who seek to measure the value and the effect of such sketches have an easy task before them. They only need to strike out their titles.[31]

27. 'Trios for Pianoforte, Violin and Violoncello,' in *Neue Zeitschrift für Musik*, 1842.

28. 'Pianoforte Music,' in *Neue Zeitschrift für Musik*, 1842.

29. 'Three Prize Sonatas,' in *Neue Zeitschrift für Musik*, 1842.

30. 'Etudes for the Pianoforte,' in *Neue Zeitschrift für Musik*, 1842.

31. 'Pianoforte Music,' in *Neue Zeitschrift für Musik*, 1842.

1843

How beautiful a period in a young artist's life is that, when, untroubled by a thought of the time or fame, he lives for his ideal only, willing to sacrifice everything to his art, treating the smallest details with the closest industry![32]

32. 'Song and Lied,' in *Neue Zeitschrift für Musik*, 1843.

Chapter Three

Schumann on the Public and Posterity

1832

The public, which forgets so easily, seldom overlooks anything really remarkable, though I am sometimes tempted to compare it to a herd of cattle momentarily distracted by the lightening from its peaceful grazing.[1]

You are quite right to insist that every man should aim at contributing to the common weal; but, let me add he must not sink to the common level. Climbing brings us to the top of the ladder. I have no desire to be understood by the common herd.[2]

1833

The characteristic of the extraordinary is that it cannot always be understood. The majority understand best what is superficial-virtuoso music, for example …

People say, 'It pleased' or 'It did not please,' as if there were nothing higher than the art of pleasing the public! …

How deeply moved I feel, when an artist—whose development cannot be called unsolid or unnatural receives nothing from the public for the sleepless nights he has devoted to his labor, destroying, rebuilding, despairing, here and there encouraged by a flash of genius—receives nothing, not even appreciation of the youthful faults he has escaped from! How I felt for him as he stood there, excited, sorrowful, restless, hoping for one encouraging voice! …

If you wish to understand a man, you ask him who are his friends. If you want to judge a public, you observe what it applauds, what sort of a physiognomy it presents after listening to music.[3]

---

1. Letter to Friedrich Wieck, Leipzig, January 11, 1832.

2. Letter to his Mother, Leipzig, August 9, 1832.

3. Schumann's Diary, 1833 or before.

1835

Half-educated persons are generally unable to discover more than the expression of grief and joy, and perhaps melancholy, in music without words. They are deaf to the finer shades of passion—anger, revenge, satisfaction, quietude, etc. Therefore it is difficult for them to understand great masters like Schubert and Beethoven, who have translated almost every possible condition of life into music ...

So, so, my public, I have you again! Once more we can harass each other. How long have I not desired to found concerts for the deaf and dumb, to set you an example of good behavior, of which you display little, even in the finest concerts![4]

4. 'Letters of an Enthusiast,' in *Neue Zeitschrift für Musik*, 1835.

1838

Many people conducted themselves as if they thought we were doing Bach an honor, as if we were wiser than the olden time and thought it all both curious and interesting! The connoisseurs were the worst of all, smiling as if Bach had written for them—he who could have swung us all, together or separately, on his little finger—Handel, too, firm as the heavenly vault above us—Gluck, not less so. And people listen, praise and think no more about it.[5]

5. 'A Retrospective View of Musical Life in Leipzig during the Winter of 1837–1838,' in *Neue Zeitschrift für Musik*, 1838.

Clara, with your beautiful soul and your wonderful talent! You played magnificently! People don't half deserve what you give to them.[6]

6. Letter to Clara Wieck, Leipzig, September 9, 1838.

1839

We have, of course, not the slightest hope or thought of teaching the masses to understand the difference between composition and conglomeration or between the life of a master and apparent life.[7]

7. 'Etudes for the Pianoforte,' in *Neue Zeitschrift für Musik*, 1839.

A remark of yours is in my mind, about my meeting with so little appreciation. Don't be afraid, my dear Clara, you shall live to see my compositions come to be understood and be much talked about. I have no fear, and it will all get better by degrees, 'within itself.'[8]

8. Letter to Clara Wieck, Leipzig, October 10, 1839.

1840

But double force is necessary to persevere on a serious path in a large city like Vienna. Public and publishers there desire above all things light and entertaining, and a firework exhibition suits them better than a robust gladiator. So it has often happened that those who did not understand this, but struggled against the stream, have been obliged to do so alone and unapplauded, while those who abandoned their higher aim and yielded swam with a hundred others in the current and disappeared without leaving a trace behind them.

We wish the young composer perseverance enough to save him from degenerating into the latter class, for the applause of a fashionable mob is not worth the esteem of one quiet, true, exclusive artist. A public crowd is never to be satisfied, but a carefully worked out, finely finished work of art re-echoes through centuries.[9]

1842

German composers usually fail on account of their desire of pleasing the public. But let any one only give us something original, simple, deeply, spontaneously and inwardly felt and he will soon find that he can accomplish more in such a manner.

The public is apt to turn a cold shoulder to the man who is perpetually opening his arms to it. Beethoven walked about with bent head and folded arms. The crowd shrank away timidly, but gradually became familiar with, and fond of, his extraordinary speech.[10]

1843

I am told that the public takes a greater interest in my works, the earlier ones included. The *Kinderszenen* and the *Phantasticstücke* appeal, indeed, to a wide circle. Times have changed with me too. I used to be indifferent to the amount of notice I received, but a wife and children put a different complexion upon everything. It becomes imperative to think of the future, desirable to see the fruits of one's labor—not the artistic, but the prosaic fruits necessary to life.[11]

9. 'Trios,' In *Neue Zeitschrift für Musik*, 1840.

10. 'German Opera,' in *Neue Zeitschrift für Musik*, 1842.

11. Letter to Carl Kossmaly, Leipzig, May 5, 1843.

1849

I knew before the performance what the effect on the public would be, and was, therefore, not surprised. I knew also that my music would appeal to individual hearers ... In any case, I fail to see the non-recognition from which I am supposed to suffer ...

Which composer ever found an immediate circulation for all his works? And then, where is the composer whose fame is universal? Where is the work—were it even of Divine origin—universally acknowledged as sacred? I have spared no pains, it is true, but have plodded on for twenty years, careless of praise or blame, intent on proving my claim to be called a true servant of art.[12]

12. Letter to Franz Brendel, Dresden, September 18, 1849.

1851

Have you also failed to glean from my music that I do not write with the sole intent to please children and amateurs?[13]

13. Letter to J. N., Düsseldorf, September 22, 1851.

Chapter Four

Schumann on his own Creative Process

1829

I have small taste for crude theory, and have been going my own way quietly, improvising a good deal, but playing very little from notes. I have begun several symphonies, but have finished nothing ...

But if you only knew my perpetual state of ferment! Why, I might have arrived at Op. 100 with my symphonies, had I written them out ... There are times when my soul so overflows with melody that it is impossible to write anything down; at such times I could laugh in the face of any art critic who should tell me that I had better write nothing, since I cannot excel, and boldly say he knew nothing about it.[1]

1. Letter to Friedrich Wieck, Heidelberg, November 6, 1829

1830

If my talents for Poetry and Music could only be concentrated into *one* focus, the rays of light would not be so broken, and I should dare to do much.[2]

2. Letter to his Mother, Leipzig, December 15, 1830

1831

You can hardly imagine the sort of feeling it is when you can say to yourself, 'This work is yours only, no man will take this possession from you, indeed it cannot be taken from you, for it is yours only.' If you could but realize that 'only!' There is seldom any reason for this feeling, for genius comes like a flash, bursts forth in all its glory, and produces a sort of pacifying self-confidence, which need fear no criticism. During all the time I have not written to you, this feeling often came over me like a dream, from which I did not want to be awakened; but then all around me was lovely, and the world rich and radiant. If one has at last come to a conclusion and is quiet and satisfied in one's own mind, the ideas of honor, glory, and immortality, of which one dreams, without doing anything towards their accomplishment, all resolve themselves into gentle rules, only to be learned from time, life, and experience. To bring to light anything great and calmly beautiful, one ought only to rob Time of one grain of sand at a time; the complete whole does not appear all at once, still less does it drop from the sky. It is only natural that there should be moments when we think we are going back, while in reality we are only hesitating in going on. If we let such moments pass, and then set to work again quickly and bravely, we shall get on all right.[3]

3. Letter to his Mother, Leipzig, August 8, 1831

1832

I admit that the theoretical studies have done me good; for where I was once content to transfer to paper the impulse of the moment, I now stand critically aside to watch the play of my inspiration, pausing now and again to take my bearings ... There are, I think, some who, like Mozart, never experience it; others, like Hummel, steer their way through; others, again, like Schubert, never come out of it; while some can even laugh at it with Beethoven.[4]

4. Letter to Friedrich Wieck, Leipzig, January 11, 1832

You must not think I have been stagnating or idling ..., but it seems as if I could only assimilate ideas I evolve for myself, so strongly does my whole nature resent any outside stimulus.[5]

5. Letter to Heinrich Dorn, Leipzig, April 25, 1832

I compose easily and rapidly, but in working it out I am always trying all sorts of experiments, which almost makes me despair.[6]

6. Letter to Friedrich Wieck, Leipzig, June 3, 1832

My thoughts and actions are so absorbed by Art, that I am nearly forgetting German, especially how to make the letters of the alphabet. If I could only tell you everything in music, how I should astonish the world by my thoughts.[7]

7. Letter to Julius Schumann, Leipzig, July 18, 1832

I am working hard at my symphony ... Of course, in instrumenting the first movement, I often put in yellow instead of blue; but I consider this art so difficult that it will take long years' study to give one certainty and self-control.[8]

8. Letter to Hofmeister, Zwickau, December 17, 1832

1833

My work is probably doomed to remain a ruin, like many another, as the only progress I have made of late is in scratching out.⁹

9. Letter to Clara Wieck, Leipzig, August 2, 1833

1834

I have always been very strict as regards themes, because the entire construction depends upon them.¹⁰

10. Letter to Hauptmann von Fricken, Leipzig, September, 1834

1835

Many look too seriously at the difficult- question as to how far instrumental music dare venture in the attempted realization of thoughts and events. People err when they suppose that composers prepare pens and paper with the deliberate predetermination of sketching, painting, expressing this or that. Yet we must not estimate outward influences and impressions too lightly. Involuntarily an idea sometimes develops itself simultaneously with the musical imagination; the eye is awake as well as the ear, and this ever busy organ sometimes holds fast to certain outlines amid all the sounds and tones, which, keeping pace with the music, form and condense into clear shapes. The more elements congenially related to music which the thought or picture created in tones contains within it, the more poetic and plastic will be the expression of the composition; and in proportion to the imaginativeness and keenness of the musician in receiving these impressions will be the elevating and touching power of his work.¹¹

11. 'Symphony by Hector Berlioz,' in *Neue Zeitschrift für Musik*, 1835

1838

The process by means of which the composer selects this or that principal key for the expression of his feelings is as little explainable as the creative process of genius itself, which chooses a certain form as the vehicle in which to enclose a thought with certainty. The composer will select the right key without more reflection than the painter employs in choosing his colors.¹²

12. 'Characteristics of Tonality,' in *Neue Zeitschrift für Musik*, 1835

1838

If I am not mistaken, [the symphony] pleased so little on its first performance in Vienna, that Cherubini refused to publish it, and afterwards transformed it into a quartet. And thus a double failure has arisen; for if the music, as a symphony, sounded too much like a quartet, the quartet is too symphonic. I am opposed to all such remolding; it seems to me an offence against the divine first inspiration.[13]

13. 'Sixth Quartet Morning,' in *Neue Zeitschrift für Musik*, 1838

We welcome sympathy from any quarter, but how much more heartily from the genuine art-lover, who is indeed, rare as the genuine artist himself! Then, too, I feel that my path is fairly solitary; no acclaiming crowd inspires me to fresh effort, but I keep my eyes fixed on my great examples, Bach and Beethoven, whose far-off images give unfailing help and encouragement ... You have still to expect my best work; for I am conscious of a certain inward strength.[14]

14. Letter to Simonin de Sire, Leipzig, February 8, 1838

Altogether, I am glad to see that my compositions are making their way here and there, and my style is far more free and clear, and, I think, more graceful. In fact, for the last year and a half, I have felt as though I possessed a secret.[15]

15. Letter to Clara Wieck, Leipzig, February 11, 1838

The piano is getting too limited for me. In my latest compositions I often hear many things that I can hardly explain. It is most extraordinary how I write almost everything in canon, and then only detect the imitation afterwards, and often find inversions, rhythms in contrary motion, etc. I am paying great attention to melody now ... But of course by 'melody'' I mean something different from Italian airs, which always seem to me like the songs of birds, pretty to listen to, but without any depth or meaning.[16]

16. Letter to Clara Wieck, Leipzig, March, 1838

I have discovered that suspense and longing are the best spurs to the imagination. I have had my full share of these the last few days, as I sat waiting for your letter and writing whole volumes of wonderful, crazy, gay compositions, which will make you open your eyes when you play them. Indeed, I sometimes feel as if I should burst with music.[17]

17. Letter to Clara Wieck, Leipzig, March 17–19, 1838

How full of music I am now, and always such lovely melodies! ... Even to myself my music now seems wonderfully intricate in spite of its simplicity; its eloquence comes straight from the heart, and every one is affected when I play before people, as I often do now, and like to do ...

I am affected by everything that goes on in the world, and think it all over in my own way, politics, literature, and people, and then I long to express my feelings and find an outlet for them in music. That is why my compositions are sometimes difficult to understand, because they are connected with distant interests; and sometimes striking, because everything extraordinary that happens impresses me, and impels me to express it in music. And that is why so few modern compositions satisfy me, because, apart from all their faults of construction, they deal in musical sentiment of the lowest order, and in commonplace lyrical effusions. The best of what is done here does not equal my earliest musical efforts. Theirs may be a flower, but mine is a poem, and infinitely more spiritual; theirs is a mere natural impulse, mine the result of poetical consciousness. I do not realize all this while I am composing; it only comes to me afterwards ... And I cannot talk about it; in fact, I can only speak of music in broken sentences, although I think a great deal about it.[18]

18. Letter to Clara Wieck, Leipzig, April 13, 1838

I have also completed ten considerable compositions within these two years. There is heart's blood in them, too![19]

19. Letter to Clara Wieck, Leipzig, May 10, 1838

I have composed very little here; I seem to have lost the art. But I have been through that stage before, and know that I shall work all the better after it.[20]

20. Letter to Clara Wieck, Vienna, December 3, 1838

1839

For so delicately organized is a musician's imagination, that, let him once lose the trace of a creative idea, let but a short period of time cover it, and only the happiest accident of the rarest moment can again recover it; therefore a work, once interrupted and laid aside, is seldom a perfect one; it is then better for the composer to begin a new one, and to forget the previous mood entirely.[21]

21. 'Sonatas for Pianoforte,' in *Neue Zeitschrift für Musik*, 1839

Some traces of the battles I have had to fight on Clara's account may perhaps be discernible in my music, and you will not fail to comprehend them. The concerto, the sonata, the *Davidsbündler* dances, the *Kreisleriana*, and the *Novelettes*, may be said to have been almost entirely inspired by her.[22]

22. Letter to H. Dorn, Leipzig, September, 1839

1840

When I consider that my music has nothing mechanical about it, but makes inconceivable demands on my heart, it seems only natural that the heart should need rest after such exertions ... I am doing nothing but vocal music of all sorts just now, including some quartets for male voices ... I can hardly describe to you the pleasure of vocal—as compared with instrumental—writing, and the tempest of ideas that surges within me as I sit at work. I have had some entirely new ideas, and am even meditating an opera, though that is impossible so long as I edit the paper.[23]

But his world is not mine, Clärchen. Art, as we know it—you when you play, I when I compose—has an intimate charm that is worth more to me than all Liszt's splendor and tinsel![24]

I feel so well and brisk that I work almost without knowing it.[25]

I have been composing so much that I wonder at myself. But I cannot help it. I could sing myself to death, like a nightingale. I have finished the twelve Eichendorff songs, and forgotten them in the stress of beginning new work.[26]

You will be amazed to see the quantity of work I have finished in this short time. There is only the copying left to do. But it is high time I stopped, and I cannot ... Composing is making me forget how to write or think; my letters prove it. Oh, why did I not realize earlier that music was my sole vocation?

I have actually reached Op. 22. I should never have thought that, when I was at Op. 1. In eight years 22 compositions are about enough; now I will write twice as much again, and then die. Sometimes I feel as if I were finding out quite new ways in music.[27]

The years that have intervened since I last wrote have been extremely eventful ... You will find many of my struggles reflected in my compositions.[28]

23. Letter to Gustav Keferstein, Leipzig, February 8, 1840

24. Letter to Clara Wieck, Leipzig, March 18, 1840

25. Letter to Clara Wieck, Leipzig, May 10, 1840

26. Letter to Clara Wieck, Leipzig, May 15, 1840

27. Letter to Clara Wieck, Leipzig, May 31, 1840

28. Letter to Camille Stamaty, Leipzig, September 28, 1840

1843

Philosophers imagine the question to be worse than it is; they are certainly mistaken in supposing that a composer who works according to an idea, sets himself down like a preacher on Saturday afternoon, portions out his task in the customary three parts, and works it up accordingly. The creative imagination of a musician is something very different, and though a picture, an idea, may float before him, he is only then happy in his labor when this idea comes to him clothed in lovely melodies, and borne by the same invisible hands that bore the 'golden bucket,' spoken of somewhere by Goethe.[29]

[My compositions] reflect for the most part the stormy scenes of my early life. The man and the musician in me have always struggled to manifest themselves simultaneously; indeed, this is still the case, although I have attained some degree of mastery over both.[30]

1845

For days my head has been a whirl of drums and trumpets (Trombe in C). I don't know what will come of it.[31]

1849

If you will examine my compositions, you cannot fail to find a considerable amount of variety in them, for I have always sought to make each one fresh, not only in form, but in idea. And really, you know, our little group at Leipzig was not so bad, including as it did Mendelssohn, Hiller, and Bennett; at least, we did not compare unfavorably with the Parisians, Viennese, and Berliners. If a common trait distinguishes our compositions as a group, call it philistinism or what you will, all artistic epochs show a similar phenomenon. Take Bach, Handel and Gluck, or Mozart, Haydn and Beethoven, respectively and you will find a hundred instances of perplexing similarity in their work. I must except Beethoven's last compositions, although they again revert to Bach. No one is entirely original.[32]

1851

My chief endeavor was to arrive at clearness as to the musical form. We have such a mass of material that it will need careful sifting. We must reject all that is not essential to the development … [33]

29. 'Symphonies for Orchestra,' in *Neue Zeitschrift für Musik*, 1843

30. Letter to Carl Kossmaly regarding his early compositions, Leipzig, May 5, 1843

31. Letter to Mendelssohn, Dresden, September, 1845

32. Letter to Liszt, Bad Kreischa, near Dresden, May 31, 1849

33. Letter to R. Pohl, on the plans for an oratorio on Luther, Düsseldorf, February 14, 1851

Chapter Five

Schumann On His Own Compositions

Thème sur le nom Abegg, varié pour le pianoforte, Op. 1
[1829–1830]

1831

I shall shortly become the father of a fine, healthy infant, whom I should like to see christened before I leave Leipzig. How I hope you will understand its child's message of youth and life! If you did but know the first joys of authorship! What hopes and prophetic visions fill my soul's heaven! Is it not a consoling thought that this first leaf of my imagination which flutters into ether may find its way to some sore heart, bringing balm to soothe its pain and heal its wound?[1]

1. Letter to his Mother, Leipzig, September 21, 1831

Papillons, Op. 2
[1829–1831]

1832

Tell [my family] to read the last scene in Jean Paul's 'Flegeljahre' as soon as possible, because the Papillons are intended as a musical representation of that masquerade; and then ask them if they can find anything there reflecting Wina's angelic love, Walt's poetical nature, or Vult's sparkling intellect.[2]

2. Letter to his family, Leipzig, April 17, 1832

Because I consider you a poet and a kindred spirit with Jean Paul, I am now going to add a few words about the origin of the Papillons, as the thread which connects them is a very slender one indeed. You may remember the last scenes in the 'Flegeljahre,' with the 'Larventanz,' 'Walt,' 'Vult,' 'Masks,' 'Wina,' 'Vult' s Dances,' 'The Exchange of Masks,' 'Confessions,' 'Anger,' 'Discoveries,' the hurrying away, the concluding scene, and the departing brother. I often turned to the last page, for the end seemed like a fresh beginning, and almost unconsciously I found myself at the piano, and thus one 'Papillon' after the other came into existence.³

In many a sleepless night I have seen my goal before me like a distant picture, and, while I was writing the Papillons, I felt clearly that a certain *independence* was striving to assert itself, which is, however, mostly condemned by the critics. Now the 'Papillons' are fluttering about in the beautiful spring air.⁴

1834
Do not the Papillons explain themselves? It interests me to know.⁵

6 Studien nach Capricen von Paganini, Op. 3 [1832]

1832
The work was delightful, but not altogether easy, as the harmonies are often vague and ambiguous (and even incorrect), and many of the caprices are by no means perfect in form and symmetry. When one first plays through this sort of movement for a single instrument, one feels as if one were in a stuffy room, but afterwards, when one has grasped the fine spiritual threads running through it, everything grows light and beautiful, and the strange genius is made clear. But I would rather write six of my own, than again arrange three of anybody else's.⁶

6 Intermezzos, Op. 4 [1832]

1832
I have been carefully filing and polishing them, but more with a view of pleasing the artists than the public.⁷

3. Letter to the critic, Rellstab, Leipzig, April 19, 1832

4. Letter to his Mother, Leipzig, May 8, 1832

5. Letter to Henrietta Voigt, Leipzig, Summer, 1834

6. Letter to the critic, Rellstab, Zwickau, December 7, 1832

7. Letter to Hofmeister, Zwickau, December 17, 1832. In a letter to Friedrich Wieck, January 10, 1833, Schumann quotes the publisher's answer to this statement, 'Your remark quite startled me. As a man of business the opinion of the public is all-important to me, that of the critics worth nothing.'

Davidsbündlertänze, Op. 6
[1837]

1838

The *Davidstänze* and the *Phantasiestücke* will be finished in a week. I will send you them, if you like. There are many marriage motifs in the dances; they were written in the 'finest frenzy' in my experience. Some day I will explain them to you.[8]

8. Letter to Clara Wieck, Leipzig, January 5, 1838

My Clara will know how to find the real meaning of those dances, for they are dedicated to her in a quite special sense. The whole thing represents a Polterabend [an evening party, with games, before a wedding], and I leave you to fill in the beginning and the end yourself. I never spent happier moments at the piano than in composing these.[9]

9. Letter to Clara Wieck, Leipzig, February 6, 1838

You pass over the *Davidsbündlertänze* very lightly; I think they are quite different from the *Carnaval*, compared to which they are what a face is to a mask. But I may be mistaken, as I have not forgotten them yet. All I know is that they were written in happiness, and the others in toil and sorrow.[10]

10. Letter to Clara Wieck, Leipzig, March, 1838

Carnaval, Op. 9
[1833–1838]

1834
It only took me a minute to compose it.[11]

11. Letter to Captain von Fricken, Zwickau, November 20, 1834

1837
The *Maskentanz* will be child's play to you. I need hardly tell you, perhaps, that the arrangement of the whole and the inscriptions over the separate pieces were added after the music was written.[12]

12. Letter to J. Moscheles, Leipzig, August 23, 1837

1838
So your father calls me phlegmatic? Phlegmatic, and write the Carnaval, the F sharp minor sonata![13]

13. Letter to Clara Wieck, Leipzig, May 10, 1838

1839

You often play the *Carnaval* to people who know nothing at all about me. Would not the Phantasiestücke be more appropriate? In the *Carnaval* one piece always counteracts the last, a thing which everyone does not appreciate; but in the *Phantasiestücke* one can indulge oneself so deliciously.[14]

14. Letter to Clara Wieck, Vienna, January 24, 1839

1840

Here I may perhaps be allowed to make a few observations regarding this composition, which owed its origin to chance. The name of a city, in which a musical friend of mine lived, consisted of letters belonging to the scale which are also contained in my name; and this suggested one of those tricks that are no longer new, since Bach gave the example. One piece after another was completed during the carnival season of 1835, in a serious mood of mind, and under peculiar circumstances. I afterwards gave titles to the numbers, and named the entire collection 'The Carnival.' Though certain traits in it may please certain persons, its musical moods change too rapidly to be easily followed by a general public, that does not care to be roused anew every moment.[15]

15. 'Franz Liszt,' in *Neue Zeitschrift für Musik*, 1840

Phantasiestücke, Op. 12
[1837]

1838

Kragen considers 'Die Nacht' noble and beautiful, and says it is his favorite, and I think it is mine too.[16]

16. Letter to Clara Wieck, Leipzig, April 21, 1838

Symphonische Etüden, Op. 13
[1834]

1838

You were wise not to play my Etudes. That sort of thing is not suited for the general public, and it would be very weak to make a moan afterwards, and say that they had not understood a thing which was not written to suit their taste, but merely for its own sake.[17]

17. Letter to Clara Wieck, Leipzig, March, 1838

Kinderszenen, Op. 15
[1838]

1838

Whether or not in response to some words you once wrote saying I sometimes seemed to you like a child, I took flight and amused myself with working out thirty droll little pieces, twelve of which I have selected and christened *Kinderszenen*. You will like them, though you will have to forget you are a virtuoso for the time being.[18]

18. Letter to Clara Wieck, Leipzig, March 17–19, 1838

The *Kinderscenen* will probably be finished by the time you arrive; I am very fond of them, and make a great impression when I play them, especially upon myself.[19]

19. Letter to Clara Wieck, Leipzig, April 13, 1838

1839

I have seldom met with anything so clumsy and commonplace as Rellstab's criticism of my *Kinderszenen*. He seems to think I call up in my imagination a screaming child, and fit the notes to it. It is just the other way around, but I will not deny that a vision of children's heads haunted me as I wrote it. The inscriptions arose, of course, afterwards, and are really nothing more than tiny finger-posts to the interpretation and conception.[20]

20. Letter to H. Dorn, Leipzig, September 5, 1839

1840

My own work has been gayer, gentler, and more melodious in character, as I think you will see from the *Kinderazenen*. But they are mere bagatelles; I have attempted far more ambitious things.[21]

21. Letter to Camille Stamaty, Leipzig, September 28, 1840

Kreisleriana, Op. 16
[1838]

1838

Since my last letter I have finished another whole book of new things. You and one of your ideas are the principal subject, and I shall call them *Kreisleriana*, and dedicate them to you.[22]

22. Letter to Clara Wieck, Leipzig, April 13, 1838

1839

Of these [*Kinderszenen*, Op. 15; *Kreisleriana*, Op. 16; *Phantasie*, Op. 17; *Arabeske*, Op. 18; *Blumenstück*, Op. 19 and the *Humoreske*, Op. 20], *Kreisleriana* is my favorite. The title conveys nothing to any but Germans. *Kreisler* is one of E. T. A. Hoffmann's creations, an eccentric, wild, and witty conductor … The inscriptions over my pieces always occur to me after I have finished composing the music.[23]

23. Letter to Simonin de Sire, Vienna, March 15, 1839

1843

I cannot, unfortunately, lay hands on a copy of what I consider my best pianoforte works—namely, *Kreisleriana*, six *Phantasiestücke*, four books of *Novelletten*, and one of *Romanzen*. These are my last pianoforte compositions (written in 1838).[24]

24. Letter to Carl Kossmaly, Leipzig, May 5, 1843

Phantaise, Op. 17
[1836–1838]

1838

I have besides finished a Fantasie in three movements … I think the first movement is more impassioned than anything I have ever written—it is one long wail over you. The others are weaker, though nothing to be ashamed of.[25]

25. Letter to Clara Wieck, Leipzig, March, 1838

1839

You will only be able to understand the 'Phantasie' if you recall the unhappy sununer of 1836, when I had to give you up. Now I have no cause to compose in such a depressed and melancholy strain.[26]

26. Letter to Clara Wieck, Leipzig, April 22, 1839

Humoreske, Op. 20
[1838]

1839

I have been all week at the piano, composing, writing, laughing and crying, all at once. You will find this state of things nicely described in my Op. 20, the 'Grosse Humoreske.'[27]

27. Letter to Clara Wieck, Vienna, March 11, 1839

Neither does *Humoreske* convey anything in French. It is a pity that no good and apt words exist in the French language for those two most characteristic and deeply rooted of German conceptions, Das *Gemütliche* (*Schwarmerische*) and Humor, the latter of which is a happy combination of *Gemütlichkeit* and wit. But this bears out the whole character of the two nations.[28]

28. Letter to Simonin de Sire, Vienna, March 15, 1839

Nachstücke, Op. 23
[1839]

1839

I told you about a presentiment I had. It haunted me from the 24th to the 27th of March, while I was absorbed in my new composition. There is a passage in it which always kept coming back to me, somebody seemed to be sighing from the bottom of his heart, and saying 'Ach Gott!' While I was composing I kept seeing funerals, coffins, and unhappy, despairing faces, and when I had finished, and was trying to think of a title, the only one that occurred to me was 'Leichenfantasie.' I was so much moved over the composition that the tears came into my eyes, and yet I did not know why. Then came Therese's letter and everything was at once explained [29]

29. Letter to Clara Wieck, Prague, April 7, 1839. Schumann refers to the news that his brother, Edward, was dying.

Myrthen, Op. 25
[1840]

1840

Since yesterday morning I have written about 27 pages of music (something new), and I can tell you nothing more about it, except that I laughed and cried over it, with delight.[30]

30. Letter to Clara Wieck, Leipzig February 22, 1840

Das Paradies und die Peri, Op. 50
[1843]

1843

I am now engaged on a great work, the greatest I have attempted so far. It is not an opera, but, as I rather think, a new departure for the concert room. I am putting all my energies into it, and hope to finish it in the course of the year.[31]

I have finished Paradise and the Peri last Friday. It is my longest work and, I think, my best. As I wrote finis on the last sheet of the score, I felt so thankful that my strength had been equal to the strain.[32]

Genovena, Op. 81
[1847–1849]

1847

In reading your poem *Genovena*, I, as a musician, was struck by the magnificent material which it offers for music. The oftener I read your unrivaled tragedy the more vividly did I see it in its musical form.[33]

Manfred, Op. 115
[1848–1849]

1851

I hope you will like the overture *Manfred*. I really consider it one of the finest of my brain-children, and wish you may agree with me.[34]

---

31. Letter to Carl Kossmaly, Leipzig, May 5, 1843

32. Letter to Johannes Verhulst, Leipzig, June 19, 1843

33. Letter to Friedrich Hebbel, Dresden, May 14, 1847

34. Letter to Liszt, Düsseldorf, December 25, 1851

Part II

Schumann's View of the World of Music

Chapter Six

Schumann on Criticism

1833
Music induces nightingales to sing, dogs to yelp.

......

[Critics] mince the timber of the lofty oak into sawdust.

......

[Critics] are confectioners who labor for *le bon gout*, without tasting a morsel themselves who can no longer profit by *le bon gout*, because they have worked at it until they have become nauseated.

......

It is not enough that a newspaper mirrors the present; the critic must be beforehand with the times, and ready to fight for the future.

......

We yet need an organ to defend the 'music of the future.' Only such men could fitly edit it, as the great blind cantor of the Thomas school (Bach), and the great deaf Kapellmeister (Beethoven), who sleeps at Vienna.

......

Critics and reviewers are not alike; the former stands nearer to the artist, the latter to the mechanic.[1]

1. Schumann's Diary, 1833 or before

1836
A reviewer dared to say that Chopin's compositions were good for nothing but to tear in pieces. Enough! Away with your musical journals! It would be the victory, the triumph of a good one, could it bring matters so far (and many are working with this aim), that no one would read criticisms any more; and the world, from pure creativeness, would hear nothing that was written about it. It should be the highest endeavor

of a just critic to render himself wholly unnecessary (as many try to become); the best discourse on music is silence. What stupid ideas are those of music journalists regarding their own importance! They imagine themselves the idols of artists, yet without artists they would starve. Away with musical journals! No matter how high criticism aspires, it is but the poor manure of works to come; and God's blessed sun will accomplish the work far better.[2]

2. 'Critical Reviews,' in *Neue. Zeitschrift für Musik*, 1836

1839

It will be asked, To which chapter, which scene, why, and with what aim? For critics always wish to know what the composer himself cannot tell them, and critics sometimes hardly understand the tenth part of what they talk about. Good heavens! will the day ever come when people will cease to ask us what we mean by our divine compositions? Pick out the fifths, but leave us in peace.[3]

3. On Berlioz' *Waverly Overture*, in 'Concert Overtures for Orchestra,' in *Neue Zeitschrift für Musik*, 1839

Rellstab [as a critic] hardly goes beyond the ABC of music at times; chords are the only thing he understands.[4]

4. Letter to H. Dorn, Leipzig, September 5, 1839

1849

An artist who refuses to recognize honest work among his contemporaries must be numbered with the lost.[5]

5. Letter to Franz Brendel, Dresden, September 18, 1849

Chapter Seven

Schumann On Performance

On Piano Playing

1833

Experience has proven that the composer is not usually the finest and most interesting performer of his own works, especially of his newest, last created, which he cannot yet be expected to master from an objective point of view. It is more difficult for a man to discover his own ideal within his own heart, than in that of another.

......

Whether it be done out of charlatanism or daring, [playing from memory in public] is always a proof of uncommon musical powers.

......

The word 'playing' applies well here, for the playing of an instrument must be one with itself; he who cannot play with it, cannot play it at all.

......

Fingers and hands must be made easy and rapid in movement during childhood; the lighter the hand, the more perfect the performance.[1]

1834

Ask her from me to play scales every day for not more than a quarter of an . hour, but to play them all, and take them fairly fast. Without fingers there would be no art, and Raphael and Mozart could never have existed.[2]

1835

The older I grow, the more convinced I am that the pianoforte is especially prominent in three leading qualities peculiar

1. Schumann's Diary, 1833 or before

2. Letter to Hauptmann von Fricken, Leipzig, September, 1834

to it—fullness and variety in exemplification of harmony (made use of by Beethoven and Schubert), pedal effect (as with Field), and volubility (Czerny, Herz, etc.). The large, broad player exhibits the first, the fantastic artist gives the second, a pearly touch displays the third quality. Many-sided, cultured composer-performers, like Hummel, Moscheles, and finally, Chopin, combine all these, and are consequently the most admired by players.[3]

3. 'From the Davidsbündler,' in *Neue Zeitschrift für Musik*, 1835

1836

[On the Etudes, Op. 20, by J. C. Kessler] We are quite astonished to find, on so many pages, written by a composer whom we have learned to admire as a man of mind, even of poetical mind, little more than finger exercises,—dry, formal things of merely mediocre intellectual value. They are cut after such a pattern, drawn out so squarely and rigidly, that they can only be recommended as a cooling process to very imaginative play-

ers; the little additional flexibility which merely mechanical players might gain from the study of them, would be obtained at the expense of their last drop of warm blood.[4]

1839

Mastership is finally lost, through excess of study.[5]

1840

The merely mechanical artist unfortunately often loses, in the tumult of the world, his most priceless possession that ingenuous, unaffected, cheerful art-power which he sacrifices to the lower demands of the masses, until it is completely buried under the commonplace routine of life.[6]

1841

It is a great pity that pianoforte players, even cultivated ones, are generally unable to judge, or to see beyond the limits of their own finger power. Instead of first reading over a difficult piece, they bore and hack away at it, bar by bar; and then, before they have acquired even a rough idea of its formal connections, they lay it aside, and pronounce it odd, intricate, etc. Chopin (something like Jean Paul) has his apostrophes. and periods, over which it is not well to linger on a first reading, for fear of losing the principal thread.[7]

On Singing

1835

'Would that our German lady singers,' remarked Florestan, 'could recollect that they are not children—who fancy they are unseen, when their eyes are closed;—most of them hide so modestly behind their music, that one has to keep a good lookout, to catch a glimpse of the face.' Ah, how different are the Italian songtresses! When I saw them in the Milan Academy, singing at each other, rolling their fine eyes, I was almost afraid the artistic passion would make too lively a demonstration. I wish I could read something of the dramatic situation, something of the music's joy and pain, in German eyes; fine singing, issuing from an inexpressive, colorless, wooden, or marble face, leads one to doubt the existence of any inward feeling.[8]

4. 'Etudes for the Pianoforte,' in *Neue Zeitschrift für Musik*, 1836

5. 'Etudes for the Pianoforte,' in *Neue Zeitschrift für Musik*, 1839

6. 'Alexis Lwoff,' in *Neue Zeitschrift für Musik*, 1840

7. 'New Sonatas for the Pianoforte,' in *Neue Zeitschrift für Musik*, 1841

8. 'Letters of an Enthusiast,' in *Neue Zeitschrift für Musik*, 1835

1839

Such a chorus as this [one in Vienna], singing with all its physical powers, requiring rather to be softened than inspired, is very rarely to be found in North Germany, where the singers entrench themselves behind their printed parts, and are quite happy if they do not upset things altogether.[9]

9. 'Mendelssohn's St. Paul in Vienna,' in *Neue Zeitschrift für Musik*, 1839

On the Symphonic World

1838

Our musicians here [Leipzig] form a family; they see each other and practice together daily; they are always the same, so that they are able to play a Beethoven symphony without notes. Add to these a concertmaster who can conduct such scores from memory, a conductor who knows them by heart, and the crown is complete.[10]

10. 'A Retrospective View of Musical Life in Leipzig during the Winter of 1837–1838,' in *Neue Zeitschrift für Musik*, 1838

1841

I wish you knew my symphony [in B♭, Op. 38]. The performance was a great joy to me—and to others. I really think it was received with more enthusiasm than any modern symphony since Beethoven.[11]

11. Letter to Carl Kossmaly, Leipzig, May 9, 1841

1842

The symphony was written in the end of the winter of 1841. It was inspired, if I may say so, by the spirit of spring, which seems to possess us all anew every year, irrespective of age. The music is not intended to describe or paint anything definite, but I believe the season did much to shape the particular form it took. You will find it neither easy nor out-of-the-way difficult.[12]

12. Letter to Ludwig Spohr, Leipzig, November 23, 1842

1849

I wrote my symphony [C Major] in December, 1845, and I sometimes fear my semi-invalid state can be divined from the music. I began to feel more myself when I wrote the last movement, and was certainly much better when I finished the whole work.[13]

13. Letter to G. D. Otten, Dresden, April 2, 1849

On Opera

1842
What, in the way of music, do you think I pray for night and morning? German opera. There is an unworked mine![14]

14. Letter to Carl Kossmaly, Leipzig, September 1, 1842

Chapter Eight

Schumann On Music Education

Suggestions for Young Composers

1834

The idea of a varying Ritornello is very good and uncommon. It is a sort of reflection, and gives more scope to the imagination, than when one is tied down by the theme to the variations themselves, I must bring a charge against you which the modern school are rather fond of making, namely, that they are too much alike in character. No doubt the subject ought always to be kept well in view, but it ought to be shown through different colored glasses.[1]

1835

[Regarding movements with introductions] How delightful it is when Mozart—in his G minor Symphony—and Beethoven, in most of his later ones, pour out to us, from the first, full draughts of rich, foaming life. Even in some Haydn symphonies, I consider the sudden passage from the adagio to the allegro a greater aesthetic error than a hundred passing chromatic fifths.[2]

1836

Until the artist is convinced that the work he publishes will not merely increase, but will enrich the mass of other works, he ought to labor and wait. What is the use of repeating the ideas of a master—ideas that we enjoy more at their fresh source.[3]

[This Adagio] is only placed [as the second movement] because such is the custom. Sterne says that men have scarcely time enough to pull on their boots. Therefore write no more adagios, or write them better than Mozart's ...

1. Letter to Hauptmann von Fricken, Leipzig, September, 1834

2. 'Muller's *Third Symphony*,' in *Neue Zeitschrift für Musik*, 1835

3. 'Concertos for Pianoforte and Orchestra,' in *Neue Zeitschrift für Musik*, 1836

For aught I care, the fifths may ascend or descend chromatically, the melody may be doubled in every interval in octaves, but—! Yes, lately I heard (in a dream) an angelic music filled with heavenly fifths, and this happened because, the angels assured me, they had never found it necessary to study thorough-bass. Those for whom it is intended will understand my dream.[4]

4. 'Trios,' in *Neue Zeitschrift für Musik*, 1836

Away with your rules and thorough bass formulas! All your school benches had first to be cut from the cedar wood of genius. Do your duty, that is, possess talent; write what you will; be poets, be men, I beseech ye![5]

5. 'Kritische Umschau,' in *Neue Zeitschrift für Musik*, 1836

In a broad sense, every piece of music is an etude, and the simplest is sometimes the most difficult. In a narrower sense, we require a special aim in the etude; it must improve a certain technicality, and lead to the mastery of some particular difficulty, whether this lies in technicalities, rhythm, expression, performance, or what else. If many difficulties are mingled in it, it enters the domain of the caprice, it is then as well, perhaps better, to transform the etude by means of broader, inwardly connected movements like those of the concerto, which, in modern times, presents many points for study, and contains all sorts of difficulties.[6]

6. 'Etudes for the Pianoforte,' in *Neue Zeitschrift für Musik*, 1836

Beware, young artists, of baronesses and countesses, who are desirous of having compositions dedicated to them; he who wishes to be an artist, must give up the idea of becoming a lady's man.[7]

7. 'Rondos for Pianoforte,' in *Neue Zeitschrift für Musik*, 1836

1837

When a composer abjures all that might render his work more interesting, he must not wonder that others are not interested in it. Genius can sometimes afford to lay aside decorative aid, but talent needs it all.[8]

8. 'Chamber Music,' in *Neue Zeitschrift für Musik*, 1837

The best fugue will always be that which the public takes: for—a Strauss waltz; in other words, where the artistic rootwork, like that of a flower, is so beautifully concealed that we only perceive the flowers. I know a by no means contemptible connoisseur of music who mistook a Bach fugue for a Chopin etude—to the honor of both.[9]

9. 'Museum,' in *Neue Zeitschrift für Musik*, 1837

No one can forcibly attain the tender melodic vein, that, in masterworks, wanders through the most entangled labyrinth of harmony; but much is to be gained by refraining from too great a preponderance of harmony over melody, by taking special pains not to oppress the latter.[10]

10. 'Fantasias, Capriccios, etc., for the Pianoforte,' in *Neue Zeitschrift für Musik*, 1837

1838

Let me give you one piece of advice: don't improvise too much. It is such a waste of precious material. Make a point of writing everything down; you will thus collect and concentrate your ideas. You are denied the tranquility and security from interruption which are the essential conditions for finishing a composition perfectly.[11]

11. Letter to Clara Wieck, Vienna, December 3, 1838

1839

We find everything here that we dare ask from a song—poetic conception, lively detail, happy connection between voice and instrument, careful selection, insight, and warm vitality.[12]

12. 'Norbert Bergmüller,' in *Neue Zeitschrift für Musik*, 1839

He who constantly confines himself to the same forms and circumscriptions, finally becomes a mannerist and a Philistine; nothing is more injurious to an artist, than long continued repose within a convenient form; in older years the power of creation declines, and it becomes too late to make a formal change.[13]

13. 'Etudes for the Pianoforte,' in *Neue Zeitschrift für Musik*, 1839

Quick insight into errors, and complete abandonment of failures, invariably accompanies genuine talent.[14]

14. Ibid.

1840

[Fesca] does not trouble himself much about grammar, or even octaves and fifths (at least as regards the eye); he writes down what sounds well to him, and considers the ear the highest court of appeal. We have nothing to say against this principle. Whatever sounds well mocks all grammar, whatever is beautiful may scoff at aesthetics.[15]

15. 'Trios,' in *Neue Zeitschrift für Musik*, 1840

1841

Young composers can never learn too soon, that music does not exist for the fingers, but the reverse, and that no one dare be a bad musician in order to become a good virtuoso ...

Where art alone is in question, consistency, energy, strength of expression, must be increased by means of laborious striving towards improvement.[16]

1842

We should encourage every strong, manly expression in music today (when even our favorite masters too determinedly incline to the reverse). Let us not forget that but a short time ago a Beethoven lived, and said, 'Music should strike fire from a man's soul; mere sentiment will only do for women.' Few think of this; and many only endeavor to excite as much emotion as they can. They ought to be punished by being dressed in women's clothes.[17]

We do not consider the total effect of any composition would be lessened, but rather heightened, by such careful labor in detail as we find in Beethoven's works—such as the independence and vital movement of separate parts, the significant treatment of modulations (as in a passage from minor to major), the finer relations between the principal theme and the working out of other motives, etc.[18]

Keep your head clear, and play your own sonata after one by Mozart or Beethoven, and then find out where the difference lies. What the mere fingers create is nothing by mechanism; but that which you have listened to when it resounded within your own bosom will find its echo in the hearts of others, and long outlive the fragile body.[19]

1843

A fiery, good beginner always stands higher than a master in mediocrity.[20]

1846

My advice, then, is: keep your love for art; practice yourself in composition as much as possible; hold fast to the great models and masters, especially to Bach, Mozart, and Beethoven, not forgetting the present in which you live.[21]

16. 'Etudes for the Pianoforte,' in *Neue Zeitschrift für Musik*, 1841

17. 'Henry Hugh Pearson,' in *Neue Zeitschrift für Musik*, 1842

18. 'Trios for Pianoforte, Violin, and Violoncello,' in *Neue Zeitschrift für Musik*, 1842

19. 'Pianoforte Music,' in *Neue Zeitschrift für Musik*, 1842

20. 'Song and Lied,' in *Neue Zeitschrift für Musik*, 1843

21. Letter to Ludwig Meinardus, Dresden, September 3, 1846

1848

It is very nice indeed if you can pick out little melodies on the keyboard; but if such come spontaneously to you, and not at the pianoforte, rejoice even more, for it proves that your inner sense of tone is awakening. Fingers must do what the head wills; not vice versa ...

When you begin to compose, do it mentally. Do not try the piece at the instrument until it is finished. If your music comes out of your inner self, if you feel it, it will be sure to affect others similarly ...

If heaven has gifted you with a lively imagination, you will often, in lonely hours, sit as though spellbound at the pianoforte, seeking to express your inner feelings in harmonies; and you may find yourself mysteriously drawn into a magic circle proportionate to the degree to which the realm of harmony is still vague to you. These are the happiest hours of youth. But beware of losing yourself too often in a talent that will lead you to waste strength and time on shadowy pictures. You will only obtain mastery of form and the power of clear construction by firm strokes of the pen. Therefore, write more often than improvise.[22]

22. Published in 1848, together with his *Album for Youth*, Op. 68

On Teaching

1833

In every child there lies a wondrous depth.

......

[Teachers of theory] are not satisfied when a young student works out the old classic form, as a master, and according to his own understanding of it; he must do so according to theirs.

......

[To teachers of theory] If anyone, who owes nothing to your school, dares to write down anything that is not in your style, he is angrily abused. A time may come when that saying, already denounced by you as the saying of demagogues: 'That which sounds well is not wrong,' may become altered to 'All that does not sound well is wrong.'

......

The person who is unacquainted with the best things among modern literary productions, is looked upon as uncultivated. We should be at least as advanced as this in music

......

Warn the youth who composes. Fruit that ripens too early, falls before its time. The young mind must often unlearn theory, before it can be put in practice.[23]

23. Schumann's Diary, 1833 or before

1834

Method, school mannerisms, advance improvement indeed, but narrowly, one-sidedly. Ah, teachers! how ye sin against yourselves! With your school of Logier you strive to drag the bud from its sheath by force. Like falconers, you pullout your own pupils' feathers, lest they should fly too high! You should be guide-posts to point out the way, but not to run along the road yourselves also.[24]

24. 'From the Criticisms of the Davidsbündler,' in *Neue Zeitschrift für Musik* 1834

Do not give Beethoven to the children; strengthen them with Mozart, brimming with rich vitality. There are sometimes natures that seem to develop in opposition to the ordinary way, but there are natural laws which, if opposed, resemble the overturned torch, that consumes its bearer when it should have illuminated his path.[25]

25. 'Theodore Stein,' in *Neue Zeitschrift für Musik*, 1834

1836

Children and girls cannot be tormented every day with scales and finger exercises, but must be refreshed with something like a dance, at the right time. In opposition to many famous pianoforte masters, we consider as false the famous saying: 'Young players should never play dances, but Beethoven at once, where possible,' as also the fancy that they should never play anything by heart.[26]

26. 'Etudes for the Pianoforte,' in *Neue Zeitschrift für Musik*, 1836

We often hear teachers complain that there is a lack of easy pieces by German composers, and that they are obliged, consequently, to take refuge in Herz and Hunten. We recommend these miniatures [Op. 14, 23, and 24, by Taubert] to them as models of their kind, and pretty, characteristic, and naive besides, just the thing to educate a child's heart, mind, and hand.[27]

27. 'Critical Reviews,' in *Neue Zeitschrift für Musik*, 1836

1839

No one can become a master without previously becoming a scholar; even the master, indeed, is merely a superior kind of scholar, and Beethoven's Sonata in B-flat major, the uniquely great, was preceded by thirty-one other Beethovenian sonatas.[28]

Beethoven, in whose mind Nature prodigally poured the gifts that she is accustomed to distribute among a thousand. To the multitude it is, of course, a matter of indifference that Beethoven wrote four overtures to one opera, as it is whether or not Rossini gives one overture to four operas. But the artist should endeavour to follow every trace that leads him to the more secret workshop of a master.[29]

1840

Would but publishers ... make it a condition with young composers, that, before their works could be published, they should submit for inspection a correctly written volume of four-part chorales, we should then have much better capriccios.[30]

28. 'Sonatas for Pianoforte,' in *Neue Zeitschrift für Musik*, 1839

29. 'Musical Life in Leipzig during the Winter of 1838–1839,' in *Neue Zeitschrift für Musik*, 1839

30. 'Short Studies for Pianoforte,' in *Neue Zeitschrift für Musik*, 1840

Maxims for Young Musicians

The cultivation of the ear is of the greatest importance. Endeavor, in good time, to distinguish tones and keys. The bell, the windowpane, the cuckoo—seek to discover what tones they produce.

......

You must practice scales and other finger exercises industriously. There are people, however, who think they may achieve great ends by doing this; up to an advanced age, for many hours daily, they practice mechanical exercises. That is as reasonable as trying to recite the alphabet faster and faster every day. Find a better use for your time.

......

'Dumb keyboards' have been invented; practice on them for a while in order to see that they are worthless. Dumb people cannot teach us to speak.

......

Play in time! The playing of some virtuosos resembles the walk of a drunken man. Do not make these your models.

......

Learn the fundamental laws of harmony at an early age.

......

Do not be afraid of the words 'theory,' 'thorough bass,' 'counterpoint,' etc.; they will meet you halfway if you do the same.

......

Never strum! Always play energetically and never fail to finish the piece you have begun.

......

Dragging and hurrying are equally great faults.

......

Try to play easy pieces well; it is better than to play difficult ones poorly.

......

See to it that your instrument is always in perfect tune.

......

It is not enough for your fingers to know your pieces; you should be able to hum them to yourself, away from the pianoforte. Sharpen your power of imagination so that you may be able to remember correctly not only the melody of a composition, but likewise its proper harmonies.

......

Try to sing at sight, without the help of an instrument, even if you have but little voice; your ear will thereby gain in refinement. If you possess a sonorous voice, however, do not lose a moment's time but cultivate it immediately, and look upon it as a most precious gift bestowed by Heaven.

......

You must reach the point where you can hear the music from the printed page.

......

When you play, do not concern yourself with who may be listening.

......

Always play as though a master were present.

......

Should anyone place an unknown composition before you, asking you to play it, first read it over.

......

If you have finished your daily musical work and feel tired, do not force yourself to labor further. It is better to rest than to practice without joy or freshness.

......

When you grow older, avoid playing what is merely fashionable. Time is precious. It would require a hundred lives merely to get acquainted with all the good music that exists.

......

No children can be brought to healthy manhood on candy and pastry. Spiritual like bodily nourishment must be simple and solid. The masters have provided it; cleave to them.

......

Virtuoso tricks change with the times; only where proficiency serves higher purposes has it value.

......

You ought not help to spread bad compositions, but, on the contrary, help to suppress them with all your force.

......

Never play bad compositions and never listen to them when not absolutely obliged to do so.

......

Do not seek to attain mere technical proficiency—the so-called *bravura*. Try to produce with each composition the effect at which the composer aimed. No one should attempt more, anything further is mere caricature.

......

Look upon alterations or omissions, or the introduction of modern embellishments in the works of good composers as something detestable. They are possibly the greatest insults that can be offered art.

......

Question older artists concerning the choice of pieces for study; thus you will save much time.

......

You must gradually learn to know all the most important works of all the important masters.

......

Do not let yourself be led astray by the applause bestowed on great virtuosos. The applause of an artist ought to be dearer to you than that of the majority.

......

All which is fashionable again becomes unfashionable; and should you cultivate fashion until you become old, you will become a dandy whom no one respects.

......

To play overmuch in society is more injurious than advantageous. Study your audience; yet never play anything of which in your own heart you feel ashamed.

......

Lose no opportunity for making music in company with others, in duos, trios, etc. This will render your playing more fluent and sweeping. Accompany singers often.

......

If all were determined to play the first violin, we should never have complete orchestras. Therefore respect every musician in his proper field.

......

Love your instrument, but do not vainly consider it the highest and only one. Remember that there are other and equally fine ones. Remember also that there are singers, and that the highest expression possible in music is reached with chorus and orchestra.

......

As you grow older, converse more frequently with scores than with virtuosos.

......

Industriously practice the fugues of good masters; above all, those of J. S. Bach. Let *The Well-Tempered. Clavichord* be your daily meat. Then you will certainly become an able musician.

......

Seek out among your comrades those who know more than you do.

......

Rest from your musical studies by industriously reading the poets. Often take exercise out in the open.

......

Much is to be learned from singers male and female. But do not believe all they tell you.

......

Behind the mountains there also dwell people. Be modest. You have never invented or discovered anything that others have not invented or discovered before you. And even if you have, consider it as a gift from above which it is your duty to share with others.

......

The study of the history of music and the hearing of masterworks of different epochs will speediest of all cure you of vanity and self-adoration.

......

Should you pass a church while the organ is being played, go into it and listen. If you long yourself to sit on the organ bench, tryout your little fingers, and marvel at this omnipotence of music.

......

Lose no opportunity of practicing on the organ; there is no instrument which takes a swifter revenge on anything unclear or sloppy in composition and playing.

......

Regularly sing in choruses, especially the middle voices. This will make you musical.

......

What do we mean by being musical? You are not so when, with eyes painfully fixed on the notes, you struggle through a piece; you are not so when you stop short and find it impossible to proceed because someone has turned over two pages at once. But you are musical when, in playing a new piece, you almost foresee what is coming; when you play an old one by heart; in short, when you have taken music not only into your fingers, but into your heart and head. How may one become musical in this sense? Dear student, the principal requisites, a fine ear and a swift power of comprehension, come, like all things, from above. But this foundation may and must be improved and enlarged. You cannot do this by shutting yourself up all day like a hermit, practicing mechanical exercises, but by a vital, many-sided musical activity; especially by familiarizing yourself with chorus and orchestral works.

......

You should early come to understand the compass of the human voice in its four principal sorts. Listen to it in the chorus; seek to discover in which intervals lies its principal strength and through which of them it best expresses softness and tenderness.

......

Listen attentively to all folk songs. These are mines of the most beautiful melodies and will teach you the characteristics of the different nations.

......

At an early age practice reading in the old clefs. Otherwise many treasures of the past will remain hidden from you.

......

Start early to observe the tone and character of the different instruments; try to impress the tone color peculiar to each upon your ear.

......

Never miss an opportunity of hearing a good opera.

......

Highly honor the old, but also meet the new with a warm heart. Cherish no prejudice against unknown names.

......

Do not judge a composition on a first hearing; that which pleases most at first is not always the best. Masters call for study. Many things will only become clear to you when you are old.

......

In judging compositions decide as to whether they belong in the realm of art, or merely in the domain of superficial entertainment. Stand for the first and do not let the other irritate you.

......

'Melody' is the amateur's war cry, and certainly music without melody is not music. Therefore you must understand what amateurs mean by this word: anything easily, rhythmically pleasing. But there are melodies of a very different type; at whatever page you open Bach, Mozart, Beethoven, etc., they will appear to you in a thousand different guises. If you study these, you will soon tire of the monotony of modern Italian opera melodies.

......

It is very nice indeed if you can pick out little melodies on the keyboard; but if such come spontaneously to you, and not at the pianoforte, rejoice even more, for it proves that your inner sense of tone is awakening. Fingers must do what the head wills; not vice versa.

......

When you begin to compose, do it mentally. Do not try the piece at the instrument until it is finished. If your music comes out of your inner self, if you feel it, it will be sure to affect others similarly.

......

If heaven has gifted you with a lively imagination, you will often, in lonely hours, sit as though spellbound at the pianoforte, seeking to express your inner feelings in harmonies; and you may find yourself mysteriously drawn into a magic circle proportionate to the degree to which the realm of harmony is still vague to you. These are the happiest hours of youth. But beware of losing yourself too often in a talent that will lead you to waste strength and time on shadowy pictures. You will only obtain mastery of form and the power of clear construction by firm strokes of the pen. Therefore, write more often than improvise.

......

Acquire knowledge of conducting early; frequently observe good conductors; and nothing forbids you to conduct silently along with them. This will give you clarity.

......

Have an open eye for life as well as the other arts and sciences.

......

The laws of morality are also those of art.

......

You will steadily progress through industry and perseverance.

......

From a pound of iron which costs only a few pennies, thousands of watch springs worth many times more can be made. Faithfully use the pound entrusted to you by Heaven.

......

Nothing worthwhile can be accomplished in art without enthusiasm.

......

Art was not created as a way to riches. Strive to become a true artist; all else will take care of itself.

......

Only when the form is quite clear to you will the spirit become clear to you.

......

Possibly genius alone entirely understands genius.

......

Someone has declared that a perfect musician ought to be able to picture a piece which he is hearing for the first time, even the most complicated of orchestral pieces, as though he had the score before him. That is the limit of the imaginable.

......

There is no end to learning.[31]

31. Published in 1848, together with his *Album for Youth*, Op. 68

Chapter Nine

Of Foreign Lands And Peoples

Italy

1829

I declare you can have no notion of Italian music until you have heard it under the Italian skies which called it into being. In the Leipzig concert room I sometimes experienced a thrill of awe in the presence of the genius of music, but Italy has taught me to love it.[1]

1. Letter to Friedrich Wieck, Heidelberg, November 6, 1829

1836

The average Italian pianoforte compositions of our time are not worth much.[2]

2. 'Critical Reviews,' in *Neue Zeitschrift für Musik*, 1836

1838

We have lately seen young talent of all sorts of nationalities arising among us: Glinka of Russia, Chopin of Poland, Bennett of England, Berlioz of France, Liszt of Hungary, Hasens of Belgium; in Italy every spring brings forth some, whom the winter destroys.[3]

3. 'First Quartet Morning,' in *Neue Zeitschrift für Musik*, 1838

France

1840

How I wish you knew the later [compositions], particularly the songs! But you Parisians take no interest in anything outside France![4]

4. Letter to Camille Stamaty, Leipzig, September 28, 1840

Germany

1835
One must hear Italian music among the Italians; German music may be enjoyed under every heaven.[5]

5. 'Letters of an Enthusiast,' in *Neue Zeitschrift für Musik*, 1835

1836
I forgive much to a German, tastelessness, lack of order, idleness, theorising,—but never such an intentional imitation of the weakest Italian sentimentality.[6]

6. 'Fantasias, Capriccios, etc., for the Pianoforte,' in *Neue Zeitschrift für Musik*, 1836

Bohemia

1838
German towns are famed for their indifference towards persons of talent residing within their walls; others content themselves with praising their resident talent when there is question of rivalry with other towns; a third class can never cease boasting of its talented sons and daughters. Prague belongs to the last class. Whatever report we may happen to take up that proceeds from Prague, we find its home artists treated with a delicate respect, an almost maternal cordiality.[7]

7. 'Third Quartet Morning,' in *Neue Zeitschrift für Musik*, 1838

The young musicians of Prague were a great amusement to me. They are very good natured creatures, but are always talking about themselves, and praising one another's idylls and compositions, although each one thinks in his own heart that he is the best among them. I have not found a scrap of geniality.[8]

8. Letter to Clara Wieck, Leipzig, October 8, 1838

Vienna

1833
Vienna is the city in which Beethoven lived; and there is no place in the world where so little is talked about, or played by Beethoven. There they are afraid of everything new, everything that deviates from the beaten track; even in music, they object to a revolution.[9]

9. Schumann's Diary, 1833 or before

1838

Do you know that it is a long cherished wish of mine to spend some years in the city the beauties of which undoubtedly helped to inspire two great men in the noblest artistic production, the city of Beethoven and Schubert?[10]

You would hardly believe what petty cliques and sets there are here. To obtain a firm footing one needs a good deal of the wisdom of the serpent, of which, I fear, I have little. I take a great pleasure in the really admirable performances at the opera, particularly in the chorus and orchestra, of which we in Leipzig have no notion. Indeed, there can hardly be such another inspiring audience in the world; it is even too enthusiastic, for you hear more clapping than music in the theatre. It is all very gay, but it irritates me sometimes.[11]

The people here like being led, and listen attentively when anything is properly put before them, and some of the better sort actually hope for some Messiah, to whom they might offer crown and sceptre at once.[12]

To judge by my present experience, and by all that I have seen with my own eyes, it is hardly possible (owing to the oppression from above) for anything poetical, life-like, and unaffected to exist here.[13]

[Clara] makes me very happy in the midst of this material Viennese life. Here people are as gossipy and provincial as in Zwickau. I have to be very careful as a public personage of some reputation; they spy on me at every corner. I am also inclined to doubt whether there is anything more in the so-called good nature of the Viennese than a smiling face. I have not had any bad experiences myself, but I hear extraordinary things from and about other people. As for artists, I have sought them in vain; by artists I mean not simply those who play one or two instruments passably, but good all-round people capable of understanding Shakespeare and Jean Paul.[14]

1839

The Viennese generally distrusts foreign musical celebrities (except some Italian ones); but if he is once won over, he may

10. Letter to Clara Wieck, Leipzig, March 17–19, 1838

11. Letter to his family, Vienna, October 10, 1838

12. Letter to Clara Wieck, Vienna, October 25, 1838

13. Letter to Clara Wieck, Vienna, November 3, 1838

14. Letter to Theresa Schumann, Vienna, December 18, 1838

be turned and twisted in any direction—he scarcely knows where to stop with his praise, and embraces the object of it unceasingly.[15]

15. 'Mendelssohn's *St. Paul* in Vienna,' in *Neue Zeitschrift für Musik*, 1839

1840

The musician who visits Vienna for the first time, awhile delights in the festive life of the streets, and often stands admiringly before the door of St. Stefan's Tower; but he soon remembers how near to the city lies a cemetery, containing something more worthy—for him—of regard than all the city boasts,—the spot where two of the glorious ones of his art rest, only a few steps apart. No doubt, then, many a young musician has wandered like me to the Wahringer Cemetery, after the first few days of excitement in Vienna, to lay his flowery gift on those graves. Vienna, with its tower of St. Stefan, its lovely women, its public pageantry; its Danube that garlands it with countless watery ribbons; this Vienna, spreading over the blooming plain, and reaching towards the higher mountains; Vienna, with its reminiscences of the great German masters, must be a fertile domain for the musician's imagination to revel in. Often when gazing on the city from the heights above, I have thought how frequently Beethoven's eyes may have glanced restlessly over the distant line of the Alps; how Mozart may have dreamily followed the course of the Danube, as it seems to vanish amid bush and wood; and how Haydn may have looked up to the tower, shaking his head at its dizzy height. If we draw together the tower, the Danube, and the distant Alps, casting over the whole a soft Catholic incense vapor, we shall have a fair picture of Vienna; and when the charming, living landscape stands before us, chords will vibrate that never resounded within us before.[16]

16. 'Schubert's C Major Symphony,' in *Neue Zeitschrift für Musik*, 1840

Public and publishers there desire above all things light and entertaining, and a firework exhibition suits them better than a robust gladiator.[17]

17. 'Trios,' in *Neue Zeitschrift für Musik*, 1840

1842

Have not later times taught us that there are minds and master in Germany who know how to unite profundity and facility, significance and grace? Do not Spohr, Mendelssohn, and others, know how to sing, and how to write for singers?

We must point this out to the German-Italian mongrel school, which has so many adherents in Vienna. But the union is not natural; the highest peaks of Italian art do not reach much beyond the first beginnings of the German; and how can we stand firmly, with one foot on the peak of an Alp, and the other on a smooth and pleasant meadow? ...

Once the Viennese court composer was named Mozart; now it is Gaetano Donizetti,—at a salary not in precise proportion to his value. These few words will suffice to sketch the former and present musical history of Vienna.[18]

18. 'Trios for Pianoforte, Violin, and Violoncello,' in *Neue Zeitschrift für Musik*, 1842

Bach

1833

As time runs on, sources draw nearer to each other. Beethoven, for instance, did not need to study all that Mozart studied—Mozart needed to make less research than Handel—Handel than Palestrina—because these had already absorbed their predecessors. But from one source only, something new is ever to be obtained; from Johann Sebastian Bach![19]

19. Schumann's Diary, 1833 or before

1835

Again I thought how we are never at an end with Bach, how he seems to grow more profound the oftener he is heard. Zelter, and afterwards Marx, wrote excellent and striking things concerning him and yet, while we listen, we perceive that we can only very distantly approach him through a verbal description. The best illustration and explanation of his works will always be found in the music itself.[20]

20. 'Mendelssohn's Organ Concert,' in *Neue Zeitschrift für Musik*, 1835

1837

Bach's D minor concerto ... or I have always thought it one of the most admirable productions ever written.[21]

21. Letter to A. von Zuccalmag Leipzig, May 18, 1837

1838

Most of Bach's fugues are character pieces of the highest description, some of them truly poetic pictures, each of which demands its own special expression, and peculiar lights and shades. Pedantic annotations of the entering of themes will not suffice for these.[22]

22. 'Etudes for Pianoforte,' in *Neue Zeitschrift für Musik*, 1838

1839

Yesterday morning Chelard was with me for a long time and I played a lot to him. However, he does not understand much about it, and thinks Bach an old composer and his compositions old. I told him he was neither new nor old, but a great deal more, namely, eternal. I really almost lost my temper over it.[23]

23. Letter to Clara Wieck, Leipzig, October 10, 1839

1840

You said it was only by the study of Bach and Kuhnau that one could understand how Mozart and Haydn came by their music, and that it remains a mystery how the more modern composers came by theirs, or words to that effect. I cannot entirely agree with you. Mozart and Haydn only know Bach through extracts. The effect he might have had on their productive power, had they known him in all his greatness, is inconceivable. On the other hand, modern music, with its intricacies, its poetry and humor, has its origin chiefly in Bach, Mendelssohn, Bennett, Chopin, Hiller, all the so-called Romanticists (speaking of Germans only), stand much nearer to Bach than to Mozart in their music. They know Bach thoroughly, one and all. I myself make my daily confession to this high priest with a view to purifying and strengthening my musical nature. Then, again, Kuhnau must not be placed on a line with Bach, however estimable and delightful he may be. Had Bach written nothing but the *Wohltemperirtes Klavier*, he would still be worth a hundred of Kuhnau. In fact, I consider Bach to be quite unapproachable, immeasurable by ordinary standards.[24]

24. Letter to Gustav Keferstein, Leipzig, January 31, 1840

1843

You will probably not need to be told that Bach and Jean Paul influenced me more than anyone in former times.[25]

25. Letter to Carl Kossmaly, Leipzig, May 5, 1843

1849

I wonder if you agree with me that the *St. John Passion* is much bolder, more powerful and poetical, than the *St. Matthew* version? The *St. Matthew* seems to me the earlier of the two by five or six years, rather drawn out in places and of excessive length; in the *St. John* what terseness, what inspiration, especially in the choruses, and what consummate art![26]

26. Letter to G. D. Otten, Dresden, April 2, 1849

1851

My compositions—the larger works especially—might, I imagine, convince you of my acquaintance with the great masters. It is to them I go, and have always gone, for advice: to Gluck the simple, to Handel the complicated, and to Bach the most complicated of all. Let me commend you to the study of Bach; my most complicated works will thereafter seem simple enough.[27]

27. Letter to J. N., Düsseldorf, September 22, 1851

Beethoven

1833

So that genius exists, it matters little how it appears, whether in the depths, as with Bach; on the heights, as with Mozart; or in the depths and on the heights at once, as with Beethoven.[28]

28. Schumann's Diary, 1833 or before

1835

Beethoven's Sixth Symphony bears the same relation to other idyllic compositions that the true life of a great man bears to his biography.[29]

29. 'New Sonatas for the Piano,' in *Neue Zeitschrift für Musik*, 1835

Would you know all that can be drawn from a simple idea, through careful choice, industry, and, above all, genius, read Beethoven and see how he can ennoble and raise such a one aloft, until the commonest word, from his lips, becomes at length a fine and universal proverb.[30]

30. 'Critical Reviews,' in *Neue Zeitschrift für Musik*, 1835

1836

I also regret that I never saw Beethoven, that my burning forehead was never pressed by his hand,—and I would gladly give a considerable part of my life to be able to say the contrary![31]

31. 'A Monument to Beethoven,' in *Neue Zeitschrift für Musik*, 1836

1838

Beethoven's final quartets seem to me to stand, with some of Bach's choruses and organ pieces, on the extreme boundary of all that has hitherto been attained by human art and imagination.[32]

32. 'A Retrospective View of Musical Life in Leipzig during the Winter of 1837–1838,' in *Neue Zeitschrift für Musik*, 1838

I send you a few flowers from the graves of Beethoven and Schubert.

On Beethoven's grave I found a pen. Wasn't that nice?[33]

33. Letter to Clara Wieck, Vienna, October 26, 1838

1840

It should be written in golden letters, that on last Thursday the Leipzig orchestra performed—all the four overtures to 'Fidelio,' one after another. Thanks to ye, Viennese of 1805, that the first did not please ye, and that Beethoven, in divine rage therefore poured forth the three others. If he ever appeared powerful to me, he did so on that evening, when, better than ever, we were able to listen to him, forming, rejecting, altering, in his own workshop, and ever glowing with inspiration. He was most gigantic in his second onset.[34]

34. 'The Four Overtures to *Fidelio*,' in *Neue Zeitschrift für Musik*, 1840

1842

In Beethoven's later quartets treasures may be found which the world scarcely yet knows, and amid which we may mine for years to come.[35]

35. 'Prize Quartet,' in *Neue Zeitschrift für Musik*, 1842

Berlioz

1835

Yet we are often repelled by flat and common harmonies, or mistaken ones forbidden by old rules, some of which, however, sound well—unclear and vague ones, or some that sound badly, tormented, twisted. May the day in which such passages will be sanctioned never come! And yet they seem quite proper to Berlioz; and when we try to alter, improve, or take away anything, how flat one's alterations sound!

Berlioz does not try to be pretty and elegant; what he hates, he grasps fiercely by the hair; what he loves, he almost crushes in his fervor—you cannot measure him by degrees: for once let us indulge the fiery youth, who should not be measured with the retailer's yard measure! If I were to reproach Berlioz, it would be for his neglected middle parts; but they meet with a peculiar obstacle, such as we seldom remark in any other composer. His melodies are distinguished by such intensity of almost every tone, that, like some old folksongs, they will scarcely bear a harmonic accompaniment, and even seem to lose in fullness of tone when accompanied.

A born virtuoso in regard to the orchestra, Berlioz demands great requirements from the individual as from the mass,— more than Beethoven, more than any other writer. Nor does he merely demand great mechanical dexterity from the instrumentalist—he requires study, understanding, sympathy.[36]

1836

Berlioz, though he sometimes behaves himself like an Indian fakir, and slays men at the very alter, means it just as honestly as does Haydn when he offers a cherry blossom with his modest air. We can never make others accept our own belief perforce.[37]

1837

Berlioz's Francs-juges, which has been declaimed against as a monster. But I can only discover in it a well-cut, clearly sustained, but, in detail, still unripe work, by this true genius of French music; here and there it shoots forth a few lightning flashes, precursors of the tempest that thunders from his symphonies.[38]

1838

Berlioz has a human heart; he is a voluptuary full of strength and daring.[39]

1839

Other crowns seeks Berlioz, whom the Philistine dreads as a raging priest of Bacchus, a hairy monster with fiery eyes. But where do we find him today? Beside the blazing hearth in the house of a Scottish laird, among hunters, hounds, and laughing country lassies …

But the entire effect of his music possesses an irresistible charm for me, in spite of many things in it that are foreign and repellant to a German ear. Berlioz shows himself different in all his works; in each one he ventures on new ground; it is hard to know whether we should term him an adventurer or a genius; he dazzles like a flash of lightning, but he leaves behind him the smell of brimstone; he sings to us of noble truths, and then falls back into a mere student-like stammer. Many not

36. [On the *Symphonie fantastique*] in 'Symphony by Hector Berlioz,' in *Neue Zeitschrift für Musik*, 1835

37. 'The Prize Symphony,' in *Neue Zeitschrift für Musik*, 1836

38. 'Fragments from Leipzig,' in *Neue Zeitschrift für Musik*, 1837

39. 'Etudes for Pianoforte,' in *Neue Zeitschrift für Musik*, 1838

yet past the first beginnings of musical feeling and cultivation (and how few ever get beyond this!) must look upon him as insane; and he must appear doubly so to pedantic musicians by profession, who move during nine-tenths of their lives in the narrowest circles; and he dares to do things that none ventured to do before him.[40]

We have wholly missed Berlioz from the repertoire. It is true that only a few of his overtures are printed; but it would certainly not be difficult to obtain one of his symphonies—only a hint is wanting for this. But he should no longer be absent from our programs. It will be as impossible to cause him to be forgotten, by ignoring him, as to sink a historical fact in oblivion by passing it over. And the hearing of his music is a positive necessity to all who would obtain a correct judgment respecting the development of modern music.[41]

1842

Many things succeed in the first fresh start; here and there, however, the faulty schooling of the musician betrays itself, and disturbs us with a feeling such as that caused by errors of orthography in a letter that is, notwithstanding, written intelligently. Yet we must confess that we have experienced the same feeling sometimes in the case of Berlioz.[42]

Brahms

1853

I think, if I were younger, I might write a few rhapsodies on the young eagle who swooped down so suddenly on Düsseldorf from the Alps, or, to use another metaphor, the magnificent torrent which is at its best when, like Niagara, it dashes down as a cascade from the heights, bearing the rainbow on its surface, while its shores are haunted by the butterfly and the nightingale. I believe Johannes is another St. John the Apostle, whose revelations will puzzle many of the Pharisees, and everyone else, for centuries. The young eagle seems quite happy on the plain. He has found an old attendant who knows from experience how to moderate the beating of the wings without injury to his flying powers.[43]

40. On Berlioz' *Waverley Overture*, in 'Concert Overtures for Orchestra,' in *Neue Zeitschrift für Musik*, 1839

41. 'Musical Life in Leipzig during the Winter of 1838–1839,' in *Neue Zeitschrift für Musik*, 1839

42. 'String Quartets,' in *Neue Zeitschrift für Musik* 1842

43. Letter to Joachim, Düsseldorf, October 8, 1853

1853

I have begun to collect and arrange my ideas on the young eagle. Much as I should like to assist him in his first public flight, I fear that my personal attachment is too great to admit of an impartial consideration of the lights and shadows of his plumage.[44]

44. Letter to Joachim, Düsseldorf, October 13, 1853

Cherubini

1838

And now comes Cherubini, an artist who has grown grey in his own views, and in the highest aristocracy of art, the best harmonist yet among his contemporaries in spite of his age; the learned, refined, interesting Italian, whom I have often compared to Dante, on account of his firm exclusiveness and strength of character.[45]

45. 'Second Quartet Morning,' in *Neue Zeitschrift für Musik*, 1838

Chopin

1831

With the words, 'Off with your hats, gentlemen,—a genius!' Eusebius laid down a piece of music. We were not allowed to see the title page. I turned over the leaves vacantly; the veiled enjoyment of music which one does not hear, has something magical in it. And besides this, it seems to me that every composer presents a different character of note-forms to the eye; Beethoven looks very different from Mozart, on paper; the difference resembles that between Jean Paul's and Goethe's prose. But here it seems as if eyes, strange to me, were glancing up basilisk eyes, peacock's eyes, maiden's eyes; in many places it looked yet brighter.[46]

46. 'On Chopin's Variations to 'La ci darem la mano,' in *Allgemeine Musikalische Zeitung*, December 7, 1831

1835

Chopin will soon be unable to write anything more without making people cry out, at the seventh or eighth bars already, 'That is indeed by him!' People have called this mannerism, declaring that he makes no progress. They should be less ungrateful. Is not this the same original force that dazzled you so surprisingly in his first works, that in the first moment perplexed and then enraptured you? And now that he has given you a succession of rare creations, and that you understand him more easily, do you ask something different from him? That would be like cutting down a tree because it produces the same sort of fruit every year. But his productions are not alike; the trunk is indeed the same, but its fruits vary wonderfully in growth and flavor.[47]

47. 'Short and Rhapsodic Works for Pianoforte,' in *Neue Zeitschrift für Musik*, 1835

1836

As Notturnos are our subject, I will not deny that all the while I have been writing, I have been thinking of two new ones [Op. 27, in C sharp minor and D flat major] by Chopin continually; for I consider these, with many of his earlier ones, especially those in F major and G minor, as among the most heartfelt, transfigured creations that can be thought-out in music.[48]

48. 'Critical Reviews,' in *Neue Zeitschrift für Musik*, 1836

[On the Grand-Duo by Chopin and Franchomme] Whatever Chopin touches, takes his form and spirit, and even in this small salon style he asserts himself with a grace and elegance, compared to which all the finish of other brilliant writers is lost on the winds.[49]

49. 'Grand Duos,' in *Neue Zeitschrift für Musik*, 1836

How finely Chopin has realized his prophecy, how triumphantly he has issued from the fight with the ignoramuses and Philistines, how nobly he still strives onward, ever more simply and artistically! But who could have well foreseen the development of such an anomalous originality, such an energetic nature, that would rather wear itself out than submit to the laws of others?[50]

50. 'Trios,' in *Neue Zeitschrift für Musik*, 1836

Fate rendered Chopin still more individual and interesting in endowing him with an original, pronounced nationality—Polish, too; and because this nationality wanders in mourning robes, in the thoughtful artist it deeply attracts us. It was well for him that neutral Germany did not receive him too warmly at first, and that his genius led him straight to one of the great capitals of the world, where he could freely poetize and grow angry. If the powerful Autocrat of the North knew what a dangerous enemy threatens him in Chopin's works, in the simple melodies of his mazurkas, he would forbid music. Chopin's works are cannons buried in flowers.[51]

51. 'Critical Reviews,' in *Neue Zeitschrift für Musik*, 1836

1837

Imagine that an Aeolian harp possessed all the scales, and that an artist's hand struck these with all kinds of fantastic, elegant embellishments, ever rendering audible a deep fundamental tone, and a softly flowing upper voice—and you will have some idea of his playing.[52]

52. 'Museum,' in *Neue Zeitschrift für Musik*, 1837

I should never forget how I had seen him sitting at the pianoforte like a visionary seer, and how his playing seemed a dream evoked by himself, and how it was his habit, at the close of every piece, to strike the keys with one finger up and down, as if to tear himself forcibly from his dream.[53]

53. 'Report to Jeanquirit in Augsburg,' *Neue Zeitschrift für Musik*, 1837

1839

Chopin is the master of form; under his wonderfully musical figuration we can always trace a rosy thread of melody.[54]

54. 'Etudes for the Pianoforte,' in *Neue Zeitschrift für Musik*, 1839

1841

Chopin may now publish anything without putting his name to it; his works will always be recognized. This remark includes praise and blame; that for his genius, this for his endeavor. He possesses such remarkable original power, that, whenever it displays itself, it is impossible to be for a moment uncertain as to its source; and he adds to this an abundance of novel forms, that astonish us as much by their tenderness as their boldness. But, though ever new and inventive in the outward forms of his compositions, he remains the same within; and we are almost beginning to fear that he will not rise any higher than he has so far risen. And although this is high enough to render his name immortal in the modern history of art, he limits his sphere to the narrow one of pianoforte music, when, with his powers, he might climb to so great an elevation, and from thence exercise an immense influence on the general progress of our art …

Chopin was formerly strewn with pearls, spangles, and golden trinkets. He has altered and grown older; he still loves decoration, but now of that nobler kind under which poetic ideality gleams more transparently. We must allow that he possesses the most refined taste possible, but it will not be understood by thorough bassists, for they give their thoughts entirely to the detection of consecutive fifths, and every succession of these exasperates them. But even they may learn much from Chopin, about consecutive fifths above all.[55]

Liszt once said, "Rossini and Co. always close with I remain your very humble servant.' But it is otherwise with Chopin, whose conclusions almost express the contrary.[56]

This [*Tarantelle*, Op. 43] is in Chopin's most daring manner; we see the madly-whirling dancers before us, until our own senses seem to reel. We can scarcely term this lovely music; but we willingly forgive the master for the wildness of his imagination, the night side of which he may certainly be allowed to display sometimes.[57]

Czerny

1836

It is said that Mr. Czerny, surrounded by the glory of four hundred works, wrote last season to his publishers, 'that they would be glad to hear that it was now his intention to devote himself to composition.'[58]

1838

It would be hard to discover a greater bankrupt in imagination than Czerny has proved himself in his latest 'grand' work. The worthy composer should be allowed to retire on a pension, for he deserves it, and would then cease writing. It is true that the fingers of youth have much to thank him for, and he has received well deserved praise for his services in this respect. But we cannot manufacture teachers and painters, not to speak of composers, by overwhelming the world with ABC books and picture sheets; and the world and Mr. Czerny ought to know it. To be sure, gold has a pleasant ring, and publishers must live too. But the latter should not deceive themselves in regard to Czerny's latest productions; they never gave promise of a great future, and for

55. 'Short Works for Pianoforte,' in *Neue Zeitschrift für Musik*, 1841

56. 'New Sonatas for the Pianoforte,' in *Neue Zeitschrift für Musik*, 1841

57. 'Small Compositions for Pianoforte,' in *Neue Zeitschrift für Musik*, 1841

58. 'Fantasias, Capriccios, etc'., for the Pianoforte,' in *Neue Zeitschrift für Musik*, 1836

a long time they have completely failed in melodic elegance and similar qualities. In a word, he has become antiquated; we have too many of his compositions: let him have a pension![59]

59. 'Fantasias, Capriccios, etc., for the Pianoforte,' in *Neue Zeitschrift für Musik*, 1838

Dreyschack

1841

This is the first grand work [*Grand Fantasia*, Op. 12] by the young pianoforte hero who is so much talked about at present. But, unhappily, we are forced to declare that it is a long time since we have met with anything so insipid. What poverty of imagination and melody, what an expenditure in attempting to impose lack of talent upon us, what coquetry over the commonest trivialities! Had the young virtuoso no friend near to tell him the truth, no one who, overlooking his finger facility, could direct his attention to the emptiness, the nullity of his music? A private report goes about that the young virtuoso has no opinion whatever of Beethoven,—is, in fact, his declared enemy; we know nothing certain about it, but his compositions lead us to fear that there is truth in the rumor. But even if he were to study Beethoven, it would not profit him anything; he can only learn from masters of the third and fourth rank, like Strauss and Lanner.[60]

60. 'Short Studies for Pianoforte,' in *Neue Zeitschrift für Musik*, 1841

Handel

1851

You probably know Handel's *Israel in Egypt*, which is to me a model of choral composition.[61]

61. Letter to R. Pohl, on the plans for an oratorio on Luther, Düsseldorf, February 14, 1851

Lachner

1835

He is a most difficult character for the critic; not because he is too obscure and profound a thinker to be reached, but because he is so serpent-smooth, that he slips through the fingers whenever we strive to grasp him. When he has said something insipid, he makes amends by a fine expression afterwards; if he enrages us with a reminiscence of Schubert or Spohr, at once he gives us something entirely original; when we have made up our minds that all is pretentious and deceptive, he surprises us a moment later with his openness and sincerity. We find everything in this sonata that we can desire; form, melody, rhythm (where, however, lies his weakness), ease, flow, clearness, correctness; and yet nothing;, almost nothing, touches us, or penetrates beyond the ear ...

[We] expect higher things from him, when he shall have decided to sacrifice the praise of the crowd for the rarer and more precious applause of his brothers in art.[62]

1839
Lachner is indisputably the most talented and learned of all South German composers.[63]

Liszt

1838
Liszt caricatures intellectually, in spite of his occasional aberrations.[64]

1839
Opinions regarding Liszt's talent for composition vary so greatly ... here can be no doubt, however, that we have here to do with a remarkable, variously gifted, and most inspiring mind. His own life is to be found in his music ... He carried his powers as a pianist to an astonishing height, but remained somewhat behindhand as a composer; and it is probable that this disproportion will be felt even in his final works ... But I sincerely believe that had Liszt, with his eminently musical nature, devoted the same time to composition and to himself that he has given to his instrument and to the works of others, he would have become a very remarkable composer. What may yet be expected from him we can only conjecture.[65]

62. 'New Sonatas for the Piano,' in *Neue Zeitschrift für Musik*, 1835

63. 'New Symphonies,' in *Neue Zeitschrift für Musik*, 1839

64. 'Etudes for Pianoforte,' in *Neue Zeitschrift für Musik*, 1838

65. 'Etudes for the Pianoforte,' *Neue Zeitschrift für Musik*, 1839

1840

Still fatigued by a series of six concerts which he gave in Prague during an eight days' stay there, Liszt arrived in Dresden last Saturday. Perhaps he was never more anxiously expected anywhere than in the residence where pianoforte music and playing are so much admired. On Monday he gave a concert; the hall was brilliant with an assemblage of our aristocratic society, including several members of the royal family. All eyes were fixed on the door at which the artist was to enter. Many portraits of him were in circulation, and that by Kriehuber, who has most correctly seized his Jupiter profile, is excellent; but the youthful Jupiter himself, of course, interests us to quite a different degree. There is a great deal said about the prose of our day, the air of courts, the spirit of the railway, etc.; but let the right man only appear, and we piously watch his every movement. So it was with this artist, whose phenomenal accomplishments were talked of twenty years ago, whose name we have been accustomed to hear mentioned among the very first—before whom, as before Paganini, every party bowed in apparently instantaneous recognition. The whole audience greeted his appearance with an enthusiastic storm of applause, and then he began to play. I had heard him before; but an artist is a different person in the presence of the public compared with what he appears in the presence of a few. The fine open space, the glitter of light, the elegantly dressed audience—all this elevates the frame of mind in giver and receiver. And now the demon's power began to awake; he first played with the public as if to try it, then gave it something more profound, until every single member was enveloped in his art; and then the whole mass began to rise and fall precisely as he willed it. I have never found any artist, except Paganini, to possess in so high a degree as Liszt, this power of subjecting, elevating, and leading the public . But he must be heard,—and also seen; for if Liszt played behind the scenes, a great deal of the poetry of his playing would be lost. It is more easy to speak of his outward appearance. People have often tried to picture this by comparing Liszt's head to Schiller's or Napoleon's; and the comparison so far holds good, in that extraordinary men possess certain traits in common, such as an expression of energy and strength of will in the eyes and mouth. He has some resemblance to the portraits of Napoleon as a young general—

pale, thin, with a remarkable profile, the whole significance of his appearance culminating in the head. It is not this or that style of pianoforte-playing; it is rather the outward expression of a daring character, to whom Fate has given, as instruments of victory and command, not the dangerous weapons of war, but the peaceful ones of art. No matter how many and great artists we may possess, or have seen pass before us during recent years, though some of them equal him in single points, all must yield to him in energy and boldness.

Chopin stands nearer to Liszt as a player, for at least he loses nothing beside him in fairylike grace and tenderness; next to him, Paganini, and, among women, Madame Malibran;—from these Liszt himself acknowledges that he has learned the most. But I would sacrifice all the astonishing, audacious bravura that he displayed here for the sake of the magical tenderness that he expressed in the following Etude. With the sole exception of Chopin, as I have already said, I know not one who equals him in this quality. How much I hoped that he would give us some of Chopin's compositions, which he plays incomparably, with the deepest sympathy! But in his own room he amiably plays anything that is asked from him. How often have I thus listened to him in admiration and astonishment![66]

66. 'Franz Liszt,' in *Neue Zeitschrift für Musik*, 1840

I am tired out with all the excitement of the past few days. As long as Liszt is here I cannot do much work, and do not know how I am going to be ready by Holy Thursday, for I am with him nearly all day. He said yesterday: 'I feel as if I had known you twenty years,' and I have just the same feeling toward him. We have arrived at the stage of being as rude as we like to each other, and I have frequent cause to avail myself of the privilege, as he is really too capricious and has been spoilt by his stay in Vienna …

I have at last had a chance of hearing Liszt's wonderful playing, which alternates between a fine frenzy and the utmost delicacy. But his world is not mine, Clärchen Art, as we know it—you when you play, I when I compose—has an intimate charm that is worth more to me than all Liszt's splendor and tinsel![67]

67. Letter to Clara Wieck, Leipzig, March 18, 1840

I wish you could have been with Liszt this morning. He is really too extraordinary. His playing of the *Novelletten*, parts of the *Phantasie*, and the sonata, moved me strangely. Although his reading differed in many places from my own, it was always inspired, and he does not, I imagine, display such tenderness, such boldness, every day. The second *Novelletten* in D gave me peculiar pleasure. You can hardly believe the effect it makes. Will you believe that at his concert he played on an instrument of Härtel's which he had never seen before? This unbounded confidence in his own ten fingers is just the sort of thing I like.[68]

68. Letter to Clara Wieck, Leipzig, March 20, 1840

I can tell you this much, that Liszt seems to me to be more tremendous every day. This morning he played again at Raimund Härtel's, and made us all tremble.[69]

69. Letter to Clara Wieck, Leipzig, March 22, 1840

Mendelssohn

1833

There is fame enough for one man in the overture to the Midsummer Night's Dream; his other works should be allowed to bear the names of other composers.[70]

70. Schumann's Diary, 1833 or before

1835

And yet it was delightful to watch [Mendelssohn]; in his eyes we read beforehand the mental windings of the composition, and its shadings, from the most refined to the most powerful effects; like a seer he forewarned us of what was to come. How different from those Kapellmeisters who seem ever threatening to whip score, orchestra, and public with their batons! …

You should have been there, to hear and see the Mendelssohn *Concerto* in G minor played! As simply as a child, he sat down to the pianoforte, taking one heart after another captive, and drawing them along with him; and when he let them free again, we all knew that we had flown past a Grecian isle of the gods, and again alighted safely in the Firlenz concert hall.

There are some things in the world about which nothing can be said; for instance, the *C Major Symphony* with fugue by Mozart, many works of Shakespeare's, some of Beethoven's, or [Mendelssohn], when he plays his own concerto.[71]

71. 'Letters of an Enthusiast,' in *Neue Zeitschrift für Musik*, 1835

Though the Davidites have considered most of Mendelssohn's youthful works as mere forerunners of his masterpieces, yet in many of them so much originality and poetry was to be found, that the great future of this composer might yet have been foretold, with considerable certainty, by means of their promise.[72]

1836

I am almost convinced that no one can play this piece [Mendelssohn's Op. 33] with such inimitable grace as its composer, for few could wholly render its transparently shining veins, its glowing color, its changing expression of face; and I think Eusebius is right when he says the composer might make the most constant of maidens inconstant with it for a few moments.[73]

Mendelssohn is a god among men.[74]

Hardly a day passes without his producing at least one or two ideas worthy of a golden setting.[75]

1837

Mendelssohn conducted the principal events, at the head of his faithful orchestra, with the power that is peculiarly his own, and with a zeal which must be partly inspired by the kindliness that greets him on all sides. If ever an orchestra, without a single exception, believed in and depended on its director, ours thoroughly deserves praise for doing so. Of intrigues and cabals we have not heard a word.[76]

The Englishman's playing is perhaps more tender, more careful in detail; that of Mendelssohn is broader, more energetic. The former bestows fine shading on the lightest thing, the latter pours a novel force into the most powerful passages; one overpowers us with the transfigured expression of a single form, the other showers forth hundreds of angelic heads, as in a heaven of Raphael.[77]

Mendelssohn's face, which is so mobile as to reflect his own thoughts and his surroundings as well.[78]

---

72. 'Sonatas for Pianoforte,' in *Neue Zeitschrift für Musik*, 1835

73. 'Capriccios and other short Studies,' in *Neue Zeitschrift für Musik*, 1836

74. Letter to his Sister-in-Law, Theresa Schumann, Leipzig, April 1, 1836

75. Letter to his Sister-in-Law, Theresa Schumann, Leipzig, November 15, 1836

76. 'Fragments from Leipzig,' in *Neue Zeitschrift für Musik*, 1837

77. 'William Sterndale Bennett,' in *Neue Zeitschrift für Musik*, 1837

78. Letter to A. von Zuccalmaglio, Leipzig, January 31, 1837

1838

Though Mendelssohn has long been recognized as the most finished, artistic nature of our day, in all styles, whether of church or concert room, original and of masterly effect in the chorus as in the Lied, yet we believe that in this 42nd Psalm, he has attained his highest elevation as a church composer; yes, the highest elevation that modern church music has reached at all.[79]

I have not been to see Mendelssohn very often, he generally comes to me. He is certainly the most eminent man I have met. I have heard people say that he is not sincere with me. I should be very grieved to think so, as I feel that I have become very fond of him, and have let him see it.[80]

1839

Music is the outflow of a noble soul, careless whether it rises in the presence of hundreds, or for itself in solitude; but always the expression of an elevated mind. This is why Mendelssohn's compositions are so irresistible when he plays them himself; it then seems as if his fingers were an almost unnecessary means of interpretation; the ear hears, to be sure, but the heart alone is judge. I often think that Mozart must have played in the same manner.[81]

The sonata [Op. 45] is one of his latest works; would that I could—meanwhile avoiding the reproach of littleness—express in words the difference between then and now in his works. It seems as if all now sought to become more musical, more refined, more transfigured, if I do not describe falsely, more Mozartean. In the earliest bloom of his youth he worked partly under the inspiration of Beethoven and Bach, though already master of form and artistic composition; in his overtures he either leaned towards foreign poesy, or drew his subjects entirely from nature. He did so in a twofold manner, as musician and poet, and opinions adverse to this artistic leaning were expressed here and there, as well as a fear that it might become his exclusive style But this sonata is again the purest, most self-sufficing music, as fine, clear, and original a sonata as ever proceeded from the greatest of master hands, and peculiarly fitted for the most refined family circles, to be played after the reading of a Byron or Goethe poem. We may be excused from

79. 'A Retrospective View of Musical Life in Leipzig during the Winter of 1837–1838,' in *Neue Zeitschrift für Musik*, 1838

80. Letter to Clara Wieck, Leipzig, April 13, 1838

81. 'Concertos for Pianoforte,' in *Neue Zeitschrift für Musik*, 1839

saying more regarding its form and style; the sonata will be found to speak more expressively for itself.[82]

Mendelssohn I consider the first musician of the day; I doff my hat to him as my superior. He plays with everything, especially with the grouping of the instruments in the orchestra, but with such ease, delicacy and art, with such mastery throughout.[83]

David gave us, in the most admirable manner, accompanied by Mendelssohn, two pieces—priceless as compositions—from Bach's sonata for violin alone,—the same of which it has been said that 'no other part could even be imagined to it,' a declaration which Mendelssohn contradicted in the finest manner by surrounding the original with many parts, so that it was a delight to listen.[84]

1840

Mendelssohn, though he has perhaps been less influenced by it than others, still remains the child of his epoch, has also struggled, and has also heard the shallow gossip of a few narrow minded scribblers [who write], 'Music's season of bloom lies far behind us,' and has soared so high, that we may venture to say that he is the Mozart of the nineteenth century, the brightest among musicians, the one who looks most clearly of all through the contradictions of the time, and reconciles us to them.[85]

1845

They are stamped on every page with that striving after perfection which makes me look to you as my model. Then the poetry and the originality of the form! Each sonata is rounded off to a complete picture Bach's music gives me the impression of himself seated at the organ, but yours brings me a vision of a Cecilia fingering the keys. How charming that that should be your wife's name, too! The fifth and sixth struck me as being the most important. One thing is certain, dear Mendelssohn, no one but you writes harmonies so pure, harmonies ever-increasing in purity and spiritual beauty.[86]

82. 'Sonatas for the Klavier,' in *Neue Zeitschrift für Musik*, 1839

83. Letter to Simonin de Sire, Vienna, March 15, 1839

84. 'Musical Life in Leipzig during the Winter of 1838–1839,' in *Neue Zeitschrift für Musik*, 1839

85. 'Trios,' in *Neue Zeitschrift für Musik*, 1840

86. Letter to Mendelssohn regarding his organ sonatas, Dresden, October 22, 1845

Meyerbeer

1837

One is often inclined to grasp one's brow, to feel whether all up there is in the right condition, when one reflects on Meyerbeer's success in healthy, musical Germany, when one hears otherwise worthy people, musicians even, declaring that there is really some value in his music. In Il Crociato, I still counted Meyerbeer among musicians; in Robert le Diable, I began to have my doubts; in Les Huguenots I place him at once among Franconi's circus people. I cannot express the aversion which the whole work inspired in us, we turned away from it—we were weary and inattentive from anger. After frequently hearing it I found much that was excusable, that impressed me more favorably in it; but my final judgment remained the same as at first, and I must shout incessantly to those who place Les Hugenots at ever so great a distance beside Fidelio, or anything of the kind, that they understand nothing about it—nothing, nothing!

I am no moralist, but it enrages a good Protestant to hear his dearest chorale shrieked out on the boards, to see the bloodiest drama in the whole history of his religion degraded to the level of an annual fair farce, in order to raise money and noise with it. Yes, the whole opera, from the overture, with its ridiculously trivial sanctity, enrages him, to the close, after which we should all be burnt alive together as soon as possible. What is the impression left behind it by Les Huguenots? That we have seen criminals executed, and flighty ladies exposed to view. Reflect on the whole, and what does it amount to? In the first act we have an orgy of many men, with—oh, refinement!—only one woman, but veiled; in the second, an orgy of bathing women, and, among them, a man scratched up with the nails to please Parisians, with bandaged eyes; in the third, we have a mixture of the licentious and the sanctimonious; slaughter spreads in the fourth, and in the fifth we have carnage in a church. Riot, murder, prayer, and nothing more, does Les Huguenots contain; in vain we seek one pure, lasting idea, one spark of Christian feeling in it. Meyerbeer nails a heart on the outside of a skin, and says, 'Look! there it is, to be grasped with hands.' All is made up, all appearance and hypocrisy. 'To startle or to tickle,' is Meyerbeer's maxim, and he succeeds in it with the rabble. And as for the introduced chorale, which sets Frenchmen beside themselves, I declare that if a pupil brought such a lesson in counterpoint to me, I should certainly beg him to do better in future. How over-laden yet empty, how intentional yet superficial![87]

87. 'Fragmente aus Leipzig,' in *Neue Zeitschrift für Musik*, 1837

1838

I prize our own times thoroughly, and understand and respect Meyerbeer; but let anyone guarantee that in a hundred what do I say?—in the next fifty years, historical concerts shall be given, in which a note of Meyerbeers's will be performed, and I will confess that Beer is a god, and I have been entirely in error.[88]

88. 'A Retrospective View of Musical Life in Leipzig during the Winter of 1837–1838,' in *Neue Zeitschrift für Musik*, 1838

1839

[One] should cultivate his natural gifts, and not dissipate and destroy them—of which error we find so lofty a representative in Meyerbeer, the true child of his race, without home or fatherland, borrowing from all nations to feed his artistic nature at the expense of its originality.[89]

89. 'Etudes for Pianoforte,' in *Neue Zeitschrift für Musik*, 1839

Mozart

1834

Cheerfulness, repose, grace, the characteristics of antique works of art, are also those of the school of Mozart. The Greek gave to 'The Thunderer' a cheerful face, and with a cheerful face Mozart launches his lightnings. A true master does not attract scholars, but other masters. With reverence I return continually to this master, who labored so fully, deeply, broadly. Should this transparent manner of thinking and poetizing ever be supplanted by a more formless and mystic one, as Time—that casts a shadow even upon Art—may ordain, yet may that beautiful period of art never become forgotten during which Mozart reigned, and which Beethoven's mighty revolution shook to its depths, perhaps not without the acquiescence of his princely predecessor, Wolfgang Amadeus.[90]

90. 'From the Criticisms of the Davidsbündler,' in *Neue Zeitschrift für Musik*, 1834

1837

Above all, one must come into the world a Mozart.[91]

91. 'Chamber Music' in *Neue Zeitschrift für Musik*, 1837

1838

I am reported to have said at Prague: 'I could write a Mozart G minor *Symphony* in my sleep.' Some liar invented that. You know the modesty with which I approach all the great masters.[92]

92. Letter to Clara Wieck, Vienna, December 29, 1838

1843

A work of these dimensions [his *Paradise* and the *Peri*] is no light undertaking. I realize better now what it means to write a succession of them, such as, for instance, the eight operas which Mozart produced within so short a time.[93]

93. Letter to Johannes Verhulst, Leipzig, June 19, 1843

Rossini

1833

It would be one-sided in us to condemn Rossini, but that the encouragement he meets with is great, out of comparison with that bestowed on German efforts. Rossini is an admirable scene-painter; but take away the artistically managed light, and the alluring stage distance, and see what remains!

When the Overture to Leonora was played for the first time in Vienna, and almost wholly failed, it is said that Beethoven wept; in the same situation, Rossini would have laughed.[94]

94. Schumann's Diary, 1833 or before

Schubert

1829

Schubert is still my 'one and only' love, the more so as he has everything in common with my one and only Jean Paul. To play his compositions is with me like reading one of Jean Paul's novels. There is no other music which presents so bewildering a psychological problem in its train of ideas, its apparently abrupt transitions. It is rare to find a composer who can stamp his individuality plainly on such a heterogeneous collection of tone-pictures, and still rarer are those who write, as Schubert did, as their hearts prompt them. Schubert unburdened his heart on a sheet of music paper, just as others leave the impression of passing moods in their journals. His soul was so steeped in music that he wrote notes where others use words.[95]

95. Letter to Friedrich Wieck, Heidelberg, November 6, 1829.

1835

When we have labored through the rubbish that heaps itself so uncomfortably about us, such pieces [as these] bloom like oases in the desert scattered behind the music desk. We consider the sonata for four hands [Op. 30] one of the least original compositions of Schubert; indeed, he is only to be recognized here by occasional flashes. Yet for how many other composers a laurel crown would have been woven from this work alone! But in Schubert's crown it looks but like one little twig; we are so much accustomed to judge men and artist according to the standard of the best they have accomplished.

He was the most remarkable composer, after Beethoven, who, the deadly enemy of all Philistinism, practiced music in the highest sense of the word. Ye who would lament because that hand has long been cold, and can no longer answer our pressure, should remember that while such men live as he life is still worth living.[96]

96. On Schubert's piano sonatas in 'Sonatas for Pianoforte,' in *Neue Zeitschrift für Musik*, 1835. Diary

1836

Time may yet produce countless and noble things, but never again a Schubert![97]

97. "Trios," in *Neue Zeitschrift für Musik*, 1836

1838

There was a time when I talked unwillingly of Schubert, whose name, I thought, should only be whispered at night to the trees and stars. Who is not, at some period, enthusiastic? Enraptured with this new mind, whose wealth seemed to me measureless and boundless, deaf to everything that could bear witness against him, I thought of him alone. Who is the master we can esteem the same at every period of our lives? With increasing years, with increasing demands, the circle of our favorites grows smaller and smaller. The cause of this lies within ourselves as well as in them. In order to value Bach properly, we must have passed through experiences impossible in youth; even the sunlit heights of Mozart are at that time underestimated. Mere musical studies are not enough to enable us to understand Beethoven, who inspires us more in certain years with certain works. It is at least sure that equal ages exercise a reciprocal attraction on each other, that youthful enthusiasm is best understood by youth, and the power of the mature master by the full-grown man. So Schubert will always remain the favorite of youth. He gives what youth desires—an overflowing heart, daring thoughts, and speedy deeds; he tells of what youth loves best—of knights and maidens, romantic stories and adventures; he mingles wit and humor with these, but not to so great a degree that the softer ground-tone is disturbed. He gives wings to the performer's own imagination, as no other composer has done save Beethoven.[98]

98. Phantasien, Kapricen, etc., fur Pianoforte,' in *Neue Zeitschrift für Musik*, 1838

1839

Among the older composers who have exercised great influence on modern music I would draw your attention to Franz Schubert, in the first place, and also to Prince Louis Ferdinand of Prussia, two deeply poetical temperaments.[99]

99. Letter to Simonin de Sire, Vienna, March 15, 1839

Oh, Clara, I have been in paradise today! They played at the rehearsal a symphony of Franz Schubert's. How I wish you had been there, for I cannot describe it to you. The instruments all sing like remarkably intelligent human voices, and the scoring is worthy of Beethoven. Then the length, the devine length, of it! It is a whole four-volume novel, longer than the choral symphony. I was supremely happy, and had nothing left to wish for, except that you were my wife and that I could write such symphonies myself.[100]

100. Letter to Clara Wieck, Leipzig, December 11, 1839

1840

But everyone must acknowledge that the outer world, sparkling today, gloomy tomorrow, often deeply impresses the inward feeling of the poet or the musician; and all must recognize, while listening to this symphony, that it reveals to us something more than mere fine melody, mere ordinary joy and sorrow, such as music has already expressed in a hundred ways,—that it leads us into a region which we never before explored, and consequently can have no recollection of. Here we find, besides the most masterly technicalities of musical composition, life in every vein, coloring down to the finest grade of possibility, sharp expression in detail, meaning throughout, while over the whole is thrown that glow of romanticism that everywhere accompanies Franz Schubert.[101]

101. "Schubert's C Major Symphony," in *Neue Zeitschrift für Musik*, 1840

Thalberg

1836

Could the Viennese hate, they would certainly hate us for the unkind thoughts this paper has heretofore given expression to regarding the compositions of Thalberg, their darling, the very apple of their eyes. A short time ago we promised—to spare ourselves and others pain—to pass over his works altogether. To tell the truth, they make one fear that the composer felt no inward necessity to create, as if he only did it because he did not well know what else he should do; he must not, it must.[102]

102. 'Critical Reviews,' in *Neue Zeitschrift für Musik*, 1836

Wagner

1845

There is Wagner, who has just finished another opera [*Tannhäuser*]. He is certainly a clever fellow, full of crazy ideas and audacious to a degree. Society still raves over *Rienzi*. Yet he cannot write or think out four consecutive bars of beautiful, hardly of good music. All these young musicians are weak in harmony, in the art of four-part writing. How can enduring work be produced in that way? And now we can see the whole score in print, fifths, octaves and all. It is too late now to alter and scratch out, however much he may wish it. The music is no fraction better than Rienzi, but duller and more unnatural, if anything. If one says anything of the sort it is always put down to envy, and that is why I only say it to you, knowing you have long been of the same opinion.[103]

103. Letter to Mendelssohn, Dresden, October 22, 1845

I may have a chance of talking to you about *Tannhäuser* soon. I must take back one or two things I said after reading the score. It makes quite a different effect on the stage. Much of it impressed me deeply.[104]

104. Letter to Mendelssohn, Dresden, November 12, 1845

1847

Richard Wagner was stage-manager … I think I heard some of his additions to the music here and there. The ending, 'On to Troy,' was also added. This is inadmissible. Gluck would probably make use of a contrary process with Wagner's operas—he would cut out.¹⁰⁵

Were he as melodious a composer as he is an intellectual one, he would be the man of our time.¹⁰⁶

1848

Bad performance; incomprehensible tempi; under Richard Wagner.¹⁰⁷

1853

I was much interested in what you said about Wagner He is, to put it concisely, not a good musician. He has no sense of form nor euphony. You must not, however, judge by pianoforte arrangements of his scores. Many parts of his operas could not fail to stir you deeply if you heard them on the stage. If his genius does not send out rays of pure sunlight, it exercises at times a mysterious charm over the senses. Yet, I repeat, the music, considered apart from the setting, is inferior—often quite amateurish, meaningless and repugnant; and it is a sign of decadence in art when such music is ranked with the masterpieces of German drama. But enough—the future will pronounce the verdict.¹⁰⁸

Weber

1837

In the fantasia [Les adieux] to which Weber s name is attached, I hoped to refresh myself after my annoyance; but, already on the third page, I imagined every note to be cry ing out, 'I am not Weber.' And if it should be shown to me in his handwriting, yes, if he should rise from the grave himself and declare that he did write the fantasia, I would not believe it. I should heartily pity the deceived ones; but no one could rob me of my moral certainty. Papers will be probably laid before us, but they will never prove that anything is gained by the publication of a thoroughly superficial, empty piece of music, though it bears the name of the best.¹⁰⁹

---

105. 'On *Iphigenia in Aulis*,' *Neue Zeitschrift für Musik*, May 15, 1847

106. 'On *Tannhäuser*,' *Neue Zeitschrift für Musik*, August 7, 1847

107. 'On *Fidelio*,' *Neue Zeitschrift für Musik*, 1848

108. Letter to Carl von Bruyck, Düsseldorf, May 8, 1853

109. "Fantasias, Capriccios, etc., for the Pianoforte," in *Neue Zeitschrift für Musik*, 1837

1840

Weber must have been one of the most refined and intellectual of musicians.[110]

110. Letter to Clara Wieck, Leipzig, May 10, 1840

1847

We raved about this as we had not done about anything for a long time. This music is too little known and appreciated. It is Weber's noblest heart's blood, and this opera certainly cost him a part of his life—but to render him immortal by its means. It is a chain of sparkling jewels from beginning to end all intellectual, masterly. How glorious, how characteristic are some of the details ... nd how the instrument's ring! They speak to us from the profoundest, most inward depths.[111]

111. "On *Euryanthe*," *Neue Zeitschrift für Musik*, September 23, 1847

Part III
Schumann: A Self-Portrait

Chapter Ten

Schumann on his Personality and Character Traits

1828

Besides Dr. Carus, I do not visit any families. I have got rather a horror of it, and always feel miserable among people who do not understand me, and whom I cannot care for.[1]

It is a blessing for me that I do not live alone or I should easily get misanthropical. It gives me no pleasure to go to public places, and it often perfectly sickens me to see idiotic people. But yet in my own heart I am not quite so joyless, and what my fellow creatures cannot give me, is given me by music. My piano tells me all the deep sentiments which I cannot express. Ah, Mother, I have too soft a nature, I feel that; and every creature who feels so deeply must be unhappy.[2]

Every man has a great and immense longing, a nameless infinite something which no words can express. This longing awakes in the epic nature of man when he stands before ruins or the Pyramids, or in Rome, or in the Teutoburg forest, or in a graveyard. In lyric natures (of which I am one) it awakes when the sweet realms of sound are opened; or in the dim twilight, or during a storm, or when the sun is rising.[3]

I cannot and will not be weak-minded.[4]

1829

I do not see things as they are, but according to my own subjective impression, and this makes life easier and simpler.[5]

Circumstances rather than principles keep me from undue presumption, though I occasionally take a high tone with people who provoke it.[6]

1. Letter to his Mother, Leipzig, August 22, 1828.

2. Letter to this Mother, Leipzig, August 31, 1828.

3. Letter to William Götte, Schneeberg, October 2, 1828.

4. Letter to his Mother, Leipzig, October 24, 1828.

5. Letter to his Mother, Berne, August 31, 1829.

6. Letter to Friedrich Wieck, Heidelberg, November 6, 1829.

I really do feel rather conceited—not so much of my natural abilities as of my victorious strength of mind, and the consciousness that I could do better if I liked.[7]

7. Letter to his Mother, Heidelberg, December 4, 1829.

1830

You really have no notion how universally popular I am in Heidelberg, and without blowing my own trumpet too much, I may say that I am certainly much respected and liked. I have even obtained the epithet of 'the Heidelberg favorite.'[8]

8. Letter to Julius Schumann, Heidelberg, February 11, 1830.

I feel sometimes that I am not a practical person, but Providence alone is responsible for that, since it endowed me with imagination to unravel and illuminate the tangled problems of the future.[9]

9. Letter to his Mother, Heidelberg, July 1, 1830.

You are perfectly right about the cigars, but I really think I smoke less that I used. I should not go so far as to call it a passion. Last time I traveled I did not smoke fifty, and had no great hankering after them. In other ways I am retrenching as far as I can; but one extravagance remains—I still burn two candles in the evening. I hardly leave my room. I am often heavy, dull, and disagreeable; my laughter is of a sardonic order, and there is hardly a trace of my old heartiness and enthusiasm.[10]

10. Letter to his Mother, Leipzig, November 15, 1830.

I shall come before you like a vision; you must not be frightened, I am dreadfully pale, ugly and seedy-looking, and all the Zwickau ladies will be surprised and critical.[11]

11. Letter to his Mother, Leipzig, December 12, 1830.

Believe me, good Mother, with patience and *perseverance*, I can do much if I like. I sometimes lack self-confidence *before the world*, although on the other hand I can be very proud inwardly. God grant, that I may but continue to be very strong, modest, steadfast, sober. The pure natural fire always gives most beauty and warmth ... can no longer accustom myself to the idea of dying a Philistine, and it seems to me now as though I had been destined for Music from the beginning ...

This contempt and waste of money is a wretched characteristic of mine. You would not believe how careless I am—I often actually throw money away. I am always reproaching myself, and making good resolutions, but the next minute I have forgotten them, and am tipping somebody with eight groschen![12]

12. Letter to his Mother, Leipzig, December 15, 1830.

1831

The want of money can hardly throw me into either melancholy or despair, because I care too little about it, and possessing it does not affect my happiness one way or the other. But it is very depressing and uncomfortable.[13]

13. Letter to his Mother, Leipzig, February 21, 1831.

I cannot get over a certain shyness in society, and it would be just as well if I were sometimes rather more abrupt.[14]

14. Letter to his Mother, Leipzig, August 8, 1831.

I hate everything that does not proceed from an inward impulse.[15]

15. Letter to his Mother, Leipzig, November 28, 1831.

1832

I need to be with people who will draw me upward to a higher level. I am so apt to be proud and cynical with my equals or with people from whom I can admit no criticism.[16]

16. Letter to Friedrich Wieck, Leipzig, January 11, 1832.

I follow my intellectual instincts, and though I am sure I listen to the opinions of experienced men with modesty and diffidence, still I do not blindly accept them.[17]

17. Letter to his Mother, Leipzig, May 5, 1832.

Since [I am] incapable of moderation in right as in wrong doing, this self-observation or spying on my own sensations developed into a form of hypochondria, which prevented a clear conception of my future position, and was in itself depressing and unsettling. Then, too, keenly as I am attracted by art in its manifold expression and its unceasing endeavour, I was often vain enough to think that I did not play a sufficiently important part in practical everyday life. I retired still further into myself, examined my past life thoroughly, and vainly tried to arrive at some clear understanding of my aim and my scope, of what I had accomplished and of what I had become ...

Moritz Semmel, whom I respect for his discernment, resolution, and devotion to his work, proved a pleasanter companion in brighter moods; but the wide divergence of our individual aims led to a breach, the more inexplicable as we could have supplied one another's deficiencies. I was thus left more and more alone, and reached, at times, a deadlock from which I was only set free by my innate aversion to every form of idleness.[18]

18. Letter to his Mother, Leipzig, May 8, 1832.

If I am silent at times, do not think me dissatisfied or melancholy. I never talk much when I am really absorbed in my ideas, my book, or my emotions.[19]

19. Letter to his Mother, Leipzig, November 6, 1832.

1833

I have not examined myself so thoroughly for years (not even on holidays), as I did last night, after having tested the Psychometer I told you about. The whole thing, an invention of Professor Portius, is so far unexplained, but undoubtedly depends upon the magnetic interchange of metals and physical forces; but it is so interesting by its decided and finely drawn character sketches, that I came away more amazed than satisfied.

Having been brought into magnetic contact with the machine, an iron rod is given to you, which the magnet either attracts or repels, according to whether you possess this or that quality, temper, characteristic, etc., or not. My character was hit off to a 'T,' although I do not quite trust some of the good qualities. I tried in vain for the following, which amused me much:—flattering, impenetrable (like a courtier), bold, decided, heroic, boastful, envious, luxurious. My energy and strength of mind were also (very rightly) pronounced doubtful, but absolutely unpleasant epithets, such as covetous, revengeful, cunning, dogmatical, did not appear at all. But, like lightning, the magnet darted to Hypochondria (not Melancholy), and to quiet, shy, ingenious, (not dexterous, curiously enough), delicate, good-natured, obstinate, genial and original, and preponderance of sentiment. I was not made out economical any more than extravagant (want of means prevents the latter, I thought to myself). Then came indulgent, prudent, loving, intellectual, modest, (my confession is anything but that) enthusiastic, sensitive, susceptible(?), sagacious, 'meditative' (philosophic brain), noble minded, sociable, reason predominating, (rather a contradiction, the only one I detected), persevering, and sincere. Ambition and pride (perhaps virtues in a good sense), but more often weaknesses, were also excluded.[20]

20. Letter to his Mother, Leipzig, April 9, 1833.

This undertaking [the founding of the *Neue Zeitschrift für Musik*] may possibly give me the necessary basis for an assured social standing, which would be to my character what the frame is to the picture, or a vessel to its fluid contents. Like many another artist, I long to attain this, and have an instinctive distaste for an undefined position …

Now, I have a way of looking up, and not down, when I am talking, so [Clara] walks just behind me, and gently pulls my coat before every stone to keep me from falling.[21]

21. Letter to his Mother, Leipzig, June 28, 1833.

1834

The mere thought of the troubles of others is so annihilating as to deprive me of all power of action, please spare me disturbing news, or I must give up your letters. But you are mistaken if you think that I am drawing more and more into myself. Any kindly word makes me happy; I should like to thank everyone who addresses a word to me.[22]

22. Letter to his Mother, Leipzig, January 4, 1834.

1835

Except a concert, I know nothing better than the hour before one, while I hum etherial melodies at the point of the lips, cautiously walking up and down on tiptoe, and leading entire overtures on the window panes … As I stepped into the gilded concert hall, had I spoken as my face perhaps spoke, I should have said: 'Here I must tread softly, for this place is haunted by the spirits of those few gifted ones, to whom was granted the great privilege of enchanting and elevating the minds of hundreds in the same moment. There I see Mozart, stamping to a symphony, until his shoe buckle breaks; there old Master Hummel extemporizing at the pianoforte; there Catalani, angrily tearing off her shawl because a carpet has been forgotten on the platform; here Weber, Spohr, and many others.'[23]

You know me well enough to be aware how little I care about artists and how much about art.[24]

1837

I feel so lifeless, so *humilated*, today that I am incapable of a single fine thought. Even your picture is so blurred that I almost forget what your eyes are like. I am not so reduced in spirit as to think of giving you up, but so embittered by this outrage to my most sacred feelings, by being treated like one of the common herd.[25]

My pride is too strong, as you have had opportunity to judge.[26]

1838

My real life began at the point when I arrived at a clear conception of myself and my talent, and by choosing art marked out a definite course for my energies. That was in 1830.[27]

I shall also miss my native soil, fot I love this patch of earth, and am a Saxon, body and soul.[28]

It would certainly be a gratification if I could write 'Doctor' before my name. I should not have much time to give to it, as I am so pressed with all sorts of professional work. I only want it for the sake of the title.[29]

23. 'Letters of an Enthusiast,' in *Neue Zeitschrift für Musik*, 1835.

24. Letter to Dr. Topken, Leipzig, February 6, 1835.

25. Letter to Clara Wieck, September 18, 1837.

26. Letter to Clara Wieck, November 29, 1837.

27. Letter to Clara Wieck, Leipzig, February 11, 1838.

28. Letter to Clara Wieck, Leipzig, March 17–19, 1838.

29. Letter to Theresa Schumann, March 25, 1838.

I have one detestable habit, namely, showing my affection for people I love most, by playing them all sorts of tricks …

But I can be very serious too, and sometimes for days together; but don't let that alarm you, for it is only when my mind is at work, and I am full of ideas about music and my compositions …

You must not watch me too closely when I am composing; that would drive me to desperation.[30]

30. Letter to Clara Wieck, Leipzig, April 13, 1838.

I will tell you something about myself. I like being among noble and highborn people, as long as they want nothing more of me than simple politeness. I certainly cannot be always flattering, and bowing and scraping, and am quite ignorant of all tricks of manner. But where real artistic simplicity is tolerated, I feel quite comfortable, and can express myself very fairly.[31]

31. Letter to Clara Wieck, Vienna, October 23, 1838.

I feel I should like to talk to you about certain of my phases. People are often at a loss to understand me, and no wonder! I meet affectionate advances with icy reserve, and often wound and repel those who really wish to help me. I have often taken myself to task about it. It is not that I fail to appreciate the very smallest attention, or to distinguish every subtle change in expression or attitude; it is a fatal something in my words and manner which belies me … y heart is in the right place, and my whole soul is responsive to the good and the beautiful.[32]

32. Letter to Clara Wieck, Vienna, December 29, 1838.

1839

I am not fond of demonstrations of friendship either; still, where I see fine qualities, I freely acknowledge them, and if I cannot make a friend of the artist, I do of the man, and vice versa.[33]

33. Letter to Clara Wieck, Vienna, March 11, 1839.

One thing more, so that you may thoroughly understand my character. You ask me sometimes whether I could stand household worries? The only thing that could possible make me miserable would be to owe people money that I could not pay; that really would—but nothing else. I am altogether too poetical for that, though you will not find me in the least careless, and I have proved to you how exact I am in everything for your sake. I am sure you will be pleased with all my domestic arrangements. Would you believe it, the first thing I do every morning is to write down all that I have spent the day before, and calculate it to the last penny. Are you aware that since 1835 I have kept a great draft-book in which I give a minute account of every letter written and received?[34]

I am only proud with people who are arrogant without reason; real modesty, such as yours, makes me long to confess my weakness and to make myself better. My character is still unformed in some respects. I am far too restless, too childish at times, and too soft; too apt to indulge my fancies without considering other people. I have, in fact, my bad days, when there is nothing to be done with me.[35]

If you should hear anything else from Herr Wieck concerning my private life, please remember that he is exceedingly slanderous and malignant. A certain amount of dissipation in the time before I knew Clara is all I have to reproach myself with.[36]

I am inclined to agree with Jean Paul when he says that air and praise are the only things man can and should absorb incessantly.[37]

1840

I have a great favor to ask (But promise to let no third person into the secret) Clara's very considerable position in the musical world has often given me cause to reflect on my own less established footing. Convinced as I am of her disinterestedness in loving me for my music and myself alone, I still think it would please her if I attained a higher social rank. This brings me to my inquiry. Can you tell me if it is difficult to take a doctor's degree at Jena; what examination I should have to pass, if any; and to whom I can apply for information?[38]

I should like to secure my doctor's degree on one of two conditions. I could qualify for it by writing a treatise, which would be an arduous task, or the diploma might be made out to me in recognition of my past services as composer and author, which would be by far the more pleasing and satisfactory

34. Letter to Clara Wieck, Leipzig, May 19, 1839.

35. Letter to Clara Wieck, Leipzig, June 3, 1839.

36. Letter to the lawyer, Einert, Leipzig, July 3, 1839.

37. Letter to H. Dorn, Leipzig, September 5, 1839.

38. Letter to Gustav Keferstein, Leipzig, January 31, 1840.

way. I know very little Latin, but I think I should be equal to a solid German treatise. I am at present engaged in collecting material for an essay on Shakespeare in his relation to music. It is to deal with his allusions to it, his qualifying remarks, and his manner of introducing the subject in his dramas—a wide and fascinating study. In a word, I want not only to be able to say I have taken this and that degree, but to have my special claim to the honor stated in the diploma. I am told that a respected Leipzig theologian obtained a degree from your University in some such way—that is, without any dissertation, but by payment of the usual fees. Is this true?[39]

39. Letter to Gustav Keferstein, Leipzig, February 8, 1840.

I have not been for any walks yet, and look quite pale and washed out. I always feel as if I had not done enough in the world (for instance, in comparison with Mendelssohn) and that worries and irritates me sometimes, although I know that there are some who are lazier than myself.[40]

40. Letter to Clara Wieck, Leipzig, May 4, 1840.

1841

I was a little disappointed to find myself relegated to the second rank in your essay on song writers. I am anything but pleased to see myself classed with Reissiger, Curschmann, etc. My aims and my abilities are, I know, far higher, and I hope you will admit this without accusing me of vanity, which is far from me.[41]

41. Letter to Carl Kossmaly, Leipzig, May 9, 1841.

1849

It is rare to find good manners among members of any orchestra, and I know how to deal with merely vulgar, though not with rude or malicious, players.[42]

42. Letter to F. Hiller, Dresden, November 19, 1849.

Chapter Eleven

Schumann on his Health and Mental Attitude

1827

My past life lies before me like a vast, vast, evening landscape, over which faintly quivers a rosy kiss from the setting sun. I am dreaming, and before me I see arise a mighty, mighty mountain, barren and bare; upon it flowers a heavenly rose, bursting into bloom, and I long to reach it, to get nearer to it; and the mountain is steep, and the rocks frown from above …

Feelings, my friend, are stars, which can only guide you in a clear sky; but Reason is a magnetic needle, which continues to guide the ship when the stars are hidden and shine no longer.[1]

1. Letter to Flechsig, Zwickau, July, 1827.

1828

I avoid my deplorable fellow beings, I hardly know why, and very seldom go out. The puerilities of this selfish world appal me. Imagine a world without inhabitants: one vast cemetery, the dreamless sleep of death, Nature with no flowers, no spring, a broken peepshow without figures; and yet, what is this inhabited world of ours? The same: God's acre of buried dreams, the sleep of death troubled with visions of blood, a garden of cypress and weeping willow, a silent peepshow with sorrowing figures. Such it is, God knows![2]

2. Letter to G. Rosen, Leipzig, August 14, 1828.

I am rather more cheerful than usual just now; perhaps in anticipation of seeing home again.[3]

3. Letter to this Mother, Leipzig, August 31, 1828.

1829

We are relatively more cast down by failure than uplifted by success, and our appreciation of health varies according to the amount of it we possess—inversely.[4]

4. Letter to his Mother, Heidelberg, July 17, 1829.

I can never forget that evening [in Venice], when I sat weeping on the stone bench opposite the Doges' Palace, gazing wearily and sadly at the sea. Strange, unfamiliar faces passed before me, and at that moment I said to myself feelingly and forcibly: 'Among all these people passing, there is not one so utterly joyless as you, as you.'—Well, to return to Lindau, where I spent two days, rowing about on the lake, smoking, drinking, singing, and making merry, thankful once more to see honest German faces.[5]

5. Letter to his Mother, Heidelberg, November 11, 1829.

1830

If I could show you my inner self at this moment, you would see me at peace in a world bathed with the fragrance of the dawn.[6]

6. Letter to Friedrich Wieck, Heidelberg, August 21, 1830, on having decided on a career in music.

I sometimes feel quite well and happy. I work hard, and am getting on famously ...

It was only a joke about my looking pale and wretched. I am as blooming as a rose, and as healthy as a fish. I occasionally have toothache.[7]

7. Letter to his Mother, Leipzig, December 15, 1830.

1831

Poverty must be a horrible thing, because it absolutely excludes one from human society. Now that I experience it, I regret many things ... Otherwise I am not getting on so badly, and my mind and spirit are as fresh and vigorous as if a dozen fountains were playing upon them. That is due to the heavenly muse with her magic wand. I am certainly more likely to become immortal than to earn any sort of 'title.'[8]

8. Letter to his Mother, Leipzig, February 21, 1831.

I have kept in my room almost entirely for six days. I have pain in my stomach, my heart, my head—oh, everywhere! Otherwise I am in unusually good spirits. For three successive days I had to undergo a regimen of perspiration, under the doctor's orders. My hand trembles as I write. I have a touch of cholera or something of that sort; but I hope to be on my legs again.[9]

9. Letter to his Mother, May 15, 1831.

Today the sky is so deliciously blue that I should dearly love to have somebody to whom I could express how happy and summer like I feel, how my intellectual, calm, artistic life drives back all passions, and how my thoughts will often revolve round some ideal for the future for several minutes together, in short, how thoroughly I sometimes appreciate the present ...

Though I am quite well and jolly, still I dread the cholera, not so much the disease as its consequences. To be on the safe side I have made my will, but kept it as funny as possible, as I cannot imagine at all that I shall ever die.[10]

10. Letter to his Mother, Leipzig, August 8, 1831.

I must confess to you my painful, almost childish, dread of cholera, and my fear that a sudden seizure may put an end to my existence ... I have been in a fever for days, making a thousand plans, only to dimiss and revive them alternately ...

The thought of dying now [of cholera], at twenty, before I have done anything except spend money, maddens me. Altogether, I am in such a desperate state of agitation and indecision that I almost feel like putting a bullet through my head[11]

11. Letter to his Brother, Julius, Leipzig, September 5, 1831.

My holidays were so quiet that I hardly heard a sound or spoke a word. I sank into a kind of stupor, which has seized me occasionally of late years, and forthwith attacked a gigantic work which requires all my energies; and I cannot tell you how fresh, proud, and well I feel at this moment.[12]

12. Letter to his Mother, Leipzig, December 31, 1831.

1832

I am nearly always in a good humor now, thanks to Spring, the child of blossoms. But February and March are fatal months, during which I have been dull and depressed all my life. Hence my utterly inexcusable silence My consolers are Industry and Confidence. If life weighs us down today like lead, tomorrow we shall rise above it, like a butterfly over the flowers.[13]

13. Letter to his family, Leipzig, April 28, 1832.

Spring itself is at our doors, looking at me like a child with sky-blue eyes. And I am beginning to understand my existence—the spell is broken.[14]

14. Letter to his Mother, Leipzig, May 8, 1832.

In the afternoon I had been alone to Zweynaundorf, mind and heart full of happiness and bright prospects for the future. With what different thoughts I visited the same place three years ago! How undecided and uncertain I was in my manner of thinking. How much firmer and more settled I seem to be this year; my imagination and consciousness beautifully balanced, and my thoughts and feelings quite inseparable from one another ...

Edward will have told you of the singular accident I have met with [the injury to the first finger of his right hand]. This is why I am going to Dresden next Monday with Wieck. Although I go partly by the advice of my doctor.[15]

15. Letter to his Mother, Leipzig, June 14, 1832.

I cannot tell you how bravely I am making way, and how happily and industriously I work at my one object in life. The world lies so bright before me, and outward circumstances have such a beneficial influence upon me, that I have to pray my guardian angel not to make me too ambitious, and to preserve in me the childlike simplicity of a true artist.[16]

16. Letter to Julius Schumann, Leipzig, July 18, 1832.

My whole house is turned into a chemist's shop. The fact is, I began to feel uneasy about my hand, though I assiduously avoided consulting a surgeon, for fear the dreaded blow should fall in his verdict: incurable. I began to make all sorts of plans for the future—decided to study theology in place of law. In the end I went to Professor Kuhl, and asked him, on his honor, whether it would come right. After shaking his head a few times, he said: 'Yes, but not for some time—say six months.' Once I had this assurance, the weight fell from my heart, and I joyfully followed out all his instructions. They were bad enough—bathing my hand constantly in warm brandy and water by day and with herbs at night, and as little playing as possible. It is not the most charming of cures, and I fear something of the bovine element will pass into my temperament, though I confess the baths are very strengthening. Altogether, I feel so strong and fit that I have a healthy desire to thrash some one.[17]

17. Letter to his Mother, Leipzig, August 9, 1832.

I am really behaving quite nicely, and if my present steady working mood lasts, *you need have no fear for the future*. As for my hand, the doctor still tries to console me; but I have quite given up hope, believing it to be incurable.[18]

18. Letter to his Mother, Leipzig, November 6, 1832.

1833

Today I am free from the attacks. My homeopathic doctor, in whom I have now more confidence, hopes to cure me entirely in three weeks.[19]

19. Letter to his Mother, Leipzig, July, 1833.

I get thinner every day, and am shooting up like a dry beanstalk without leaves. The doctor has even forbidden me to long for anything (i.e., for you) very much, because it would be too exhausting; but today I tore the bandages off my wounds, and laughed in his face when he wanted to prevent me from writing, and even threatened to give him my fever, if he did not let me do as I liked.[20]

20. Letter to Clara Wieck, Leipzig, July 13, 1833.

What a tale I could unfold to you of sorrow and joy, lordly castles in the air, dreams of immortality and tears.[21]

21. Letter to Franz Otto, Leipzig, August 9, 1833.

You appear to have no idea of my painful disease, or you would not invite me so repeatedly. I really must try and convince you that I am anything but flourishing, as every breath of air brings on an attack. I have not been allowed out for a fortnight, and may not even wash myself.[22]

22. Letter to his Mother, Leipzig, Fall, 1833.

Not a word of these past weeks. I was little better than a statue, feeling neither cold nor heat, until, with strenuous work, some life came into me again. I am still so nervous and timid that I cannot sleep alone; but I have found a thoroughly good natured companion, and the very deficiencies of his education provide stimulus and distraction. Do you know, I had not the courage to travel to Zwickau alone for fear something might happen to me! Violent congestion, inexpressible terror, failure of breath, momentary unconsciousness—these overtake me in quick succession, though I am better than I was. If you had any notion of the lethargy into which melancholia has brought me you would forgive my not writing.[23]

23. Letter to his Mother, Leipzig November 27, 1833.

1834

Postilions have much the same sort of effect upon me as the most excellent champagne. One quite forgets that one has a head, it makes one feel so delightfully light-hearted to hear them blaring away to the world so merrily. Their merry strains seem to me like very dances of rapturous longing.[24]

24. Letter to Clara Wieck, Leipzig, 1834.

I have for some days felt fresher and better than for a long time past. Perhaps more cheerful ideas will gradually return, and then I will be so kind to everybody, as kind as they now are to me. You will find that hard to believe. The cloud-spots we think we see in the starlit sky are really radiant suns, indistinguishable to our weak sight.[25]

25. Letter to his Mother, Leipzig, January 4, 1834.

Do not worry yourself about my finger! I can compose without it; and I should hardly be happier as a traveling virtuoso.[26]

26. Letter to his Mother, Leipzig, March 19, 1834.

May the hand that opens this letter be stronger than the one that seals it! Let my health account for my long silence ... and for my flight to my native place ... I have hardly got the better of my own illness, a very depressing form of melancholia. The word is easily written, but the thing itself is sometimes beyond human endurance.[27]

27. Letter to Captain von Fricken, Zwickau, November 20, 1834.

1837

But some day I should like to tell you, in connection with this dark page of my life, the secret of a serious physical complaint I once had. It dates back to the summer of 1833.[28]

28. Letter to Clara Wieck, November 29, 1837.

1838

As early as 1833 a certain melancholy made itself felt, of which I obstinately refused to take any account, regarding it merely as the disheartenment experienced by every artist when results are not achieved with the speed he expected. I received small recognition; moreover, I lost the use of my right hand for playing. [In the same year] The death of a dear brother threw me into a state of melancholy, which gained more and more the upper hand. The news of Rosalie's death found me in this condition. In the night between the 17th and 18th of October I was seized with the worst fear a man can have, the worst punishment Heaven can inflict—the fear of losing one's reason. It took so strong a hold of me that consolation and prayer, defiance and derision, were equally powerless to subdue it. Terror drove me from place to place. My breath failed me as I pictured my brain paralyzed ... o one knows the suffering, the sickness, the despair, except those so crushed. In my terrible agitation I went to a doctor and told him everything—

how my senses often failed me so that I did not know which way to turn in my fright, how I could not be certain of not taking my own life when in this helpless condition ...

I have hardly ever been so happy as just lately. It must give you some pleasure to feel that you have brought back to life and happiness a creature who was for years a prey to the most terrifying thoughts, and had a positive genius for seeing the dark side of everything, so that he trembles as he looks back on a time when he did not value his life at a brass farthing.[29]

29. Letter to Clara Wieck, Leipzig, February 11, 1838.

My lame hand makes me wretched sometimes—here especially grows worse, too, as I don't mind admitting to you. I often bemoan my fate, and demand to know why Heaven should send me this particular trial. It would mean so much here if I were able to play. What a relief to give utterance to all the music surging within me! As it is, I can barely play at all, but stumble along with my fingers all mixed up in a terrible way. It causes me great distress.[30]

30. Letter to Clara Wieck, Vienna, December 3, 1838.

I can say that I often feel well enough here, though oftener melancholy enough to shoot myself.[31]

31. Letter to Theresa Schumann, Vienna, December 18, 1838.

1839

An evil fate has deprived me of the full use of my right hand, so that I am not able to play my compositions as I feel them. The trouble with my hand is that certain fingers have become so weak, probably through writing and playing too much at one time, that I can hardly use them. This has often depressed me, though Heaven from time to time sends me an inspiration which keeps me from thinking any more about it.[32]

32. Letter to Simonin de Sire, Vienna, March 15, 1839.

With roses and acacias in full splendor, and you, my own love, in the full bloom of your loveliness, I am indeed the most favored mortals, overwhelmed with happiness, half smothered under the load of blossoms.[33]

33. Letter to Clara Wieck, Leipzig, June 22, 1839.

1844

I have had a serious nervous illness for the past three months, and was, in consequence, forbidden every exertion, mental or physical, by my doctor. I am now a little better, and can see some brightness in life, some return of hope and confidence. I think I did too much music. My music to Goethe's Faust occupied me very much latterly, and in the end mind and body both gave way … During this time I have not been able to hear a note of music, for it was like a knife to my nerves.[34]

I am still suffering, and have moments of despondency. Work is forbidden me; I may only rest and take walks—and even these I often find exhausting.[35]

1845

Writing of any sort still tires me very much, therefore forgive me. I am already rather better. Hofrat Carus has advised early morning walks, which have done me a lot of good. Yet I am not altogether cured, and I have touches of pain every day in a hundred different places. A mysterious illness, which seems to vanish when the doctor prepares to attack it![36]

I am sorry to say that I have not yet regained my full strength; every divergence from my simple regime upsets me, and induces morbid irritability. That is why I reluctantly stayed away when my wife was with you. I must avoid every form of gaiety. There is nothing for it but to go on hoping, and that I am determined to do.[37]

1846

All exertion is forbidden; indeed, it forbids itself. I have been so ill for a long time now that I can hardly write more than one letter at a time.[38]

1849

One thing more: I was looking up Düsseldorf in an old geography the other day, and found, amongst the attractions, three convents and an asylum. I might put up with the convents, but it made me uncomfortable to read of the other. I must explain to you: some years ago, when, as you remember, we lived at Maxen, I discovered that I had from my window a full view of Sonnenstein [an asylum].

This outlook came latterly to affect me seriously—indeed, it spoilt my whole stay, and I now fear that it might be the same at Düsseldorf. I have to avoid very carefully any depressing as-

34. Letter to Eduard Krüger, Leipzig, October, 1844.

35. Letter to Eduard Krüger, Dresden, November, 1844.

36. Letter to Mendelssohn, Dresden, September, 1845.

37. Letter to Mendelssohn, Dresden, October 22, 1845.

38. Letter to Ludwig Meinardus, Dresden, September 3, 1846.

sociations of the kind. We musicians, as you are well aware, are often exalted to the heights; but the sight of the naked misery of real life wounds the more deeply. At least, this is the case with me, thanks to my vivid imagination ...

I have been suffering all this time from a headache, which kept me from working or thinking.[39]

39. Letter to F. Hiller, Dresden, December 3, 1849.

Chapter Twelve

Insights into Schumann's General Outlook on Life

Living

1831
If the life of Man is indeed a maze, one does now and then come upon the statue of a god.[1]

1. Letter to his Mother, Leipzig, November 28, 1831.

1832
Can we not have our heaven on earth if we take a simple, sober view of life, and are not unreasonable in our demands?[2]

2. Letter to his Mother, Leipzig, May 8, 1832.

1833
I love not the men whose lives are not in unison with their works.

......

It is not enough that I know something, unless I am able to make use of what I have learned, in the conduct of my life.

......

Musical curses (*diabolini*): When I turn over two pages of music at once—when a key sticks—when a doubt arises as to the time and key signature—when, in the heat of composition, no paper is at hand. But the worst of all is when the baton flies off while one is conducting.[3]

3. Schumann's Diary, 1833 or before.

Sad feelings are very attractive and strengthening to the imagination. Try to believe this, and to look into the future (which is never really so cloudy as it looks from a distance), with that bright and cheerful spirit which ought to accompany us through every age.[4]

4. Letter to Rosalie Schumann, Zwickau, January 9, 1833.

Very often what we look for in the distance lies so near that we need only stretch out our hand to seize it …

You can imagine that I am very happy and comfortable under the circumstances; and if, as I believe, outward surroundings have a direct influence on one's thoughts and actions, then I really have nothing left to wish for, unless it be that the charm of novelty may not wear off, like the delicate tints of the butterfly, which, but, for its colors, would be merely an insignificant winged insect. Seriously, though it might be said that every fresh beauty delights one for the first moment, is criticized in the second, and becomes habitual in the third, still it would be of great advantage to mankind, if the sentence could be reversed …

It is very curious, but man is far more hurt, when his inborn qualities and talents are misunderstood, than when one of his virtues is not appreciated.[5]

5. Letter to his Mother, Leipzig, April 9, 1833.

1834

Opposition only strengthens one. Every man should go his own way.[6]

6. Letter to his Mother, Leipzig, March 19, 1834.

1838

The human heart is often a strange spectacle in which sorrow and joy are strangely blended.[7]

7. Letter to Simonin de Sire, Leipzig, February 8, 1838.

Time and Aging

1828

The love of one's home and the scenes of one's childhood may become a weakness if they prevent one from being contented with the present, and only make one moan over the past.[8]

8. Letter to his Mother, Leipzig, October 24, 1828.

1829

How often man sighs, saying: 'Ah, how dreary is the present, and how beautiful was the past.' But he forgets that the past must at one time have been the present. Or one might say: 'The present is like a dream, which we only realize after we have lost it.' Or, 'How happy is old age! Two lights are reflected in the old man's face, the evening rays of this life—and the morning beams of the life to come.' Or, "How differently do youth and age contemplate life, the former full of passionate emotions, the latter calm and smiling.' If a heavy shower should darken our life, you will be the rainbow which rises above it, gently quivering, but still shining on.[9]

9. Letter to his Mother, Heidelberg, November 11, 1829.

1830

The spring has bound me up more [warmly] with myself, and has taught me to value and appreciate time, which one generally rather trifles with. Thus man alternately plays with Time, and Time with Man.[10]

10. Letter to his Mother, Heidelberg, July 1, 1830.

A clock always reminds one so unpleasantly of one's age and of the flight of time.[11]

11. Letter to his Mother, Leipzig, December 12, 1830.

Faith

1828

It would be a beautiful time if man could only let his problems rest peacefully and happily. But it is just this eternal striving of man—this great tremendous *onesidedness*, I should like to call it—which keeps fresh life in us; and that very restlessness and discontent in our strife for an *a priori* Ideal, for the highest unsurpassable maximum—is the infinite charm which binds us to this miserable existence. We can scarcely imagine the great, unfinished picture of Man in *Space*, but in *Time* the titanic giant-spirits join hands for the formation of the highest and for the gigantic work of completed creation.

Man can do everything if he wills. Then let us will, and we shall act. We live in a tremendous time in spite of the Past, and the Sphinx now smiles because she can no longer make us weep. Every question once asked of the Past we will now put to the Future, and we shall receive an answer. First of all we will purify and enlighten our own hearts—the rest will follow. Man is, as he always has been; but he might, should, and ought to be better.[12]

12. Letter to William Götte, Schneeberg, October 2, 1828.

1829

Only once in my whole life have I had an impression of the actual presence of God, of gazing reverently and unrebuked into His face; this was in Milan, as I listened to Pasta—and Rossini![13]

[13]. Letter to Friedrich Wieck, Heidelberg, November 6, 1829.

1833

Tomorrow, exactly at eleven o'clock, I shall play the Adagio from Chopin's *Variations*, and shall think intensely, exclusively, of you. Now my petition is that you will do the same, so that we may meet and communicate in spirit.[14]

[14]. Letter to Clara Wieck, Leipzig, July 13, 1833.

1836

Fate designed us for one another, as I have known for a long time, though I was not bold enough to speak to you sooner or to come to an understanding.[15]

[15]. Letter to Clara Wieck, Zwickau, February 13, 1836.

1837

We may leave the rest to our guardian angel, who destined us each for the other in our cradles.[16]

[16]. Letter to Clara Wieck, November 8, 1837.

May no one dispel these happy visions! Ah, when shall I have you for my very own! These nights of sleepless anguish, this tearless suffering endured for your sake—surely a kind Providence will one day give me compensation![17]

[17]. Letter to Clara Wieck, November 29, 1837.

1838

Providence has guided the course of events, and will continue to do so.[18]

[18]. Letter to Theresa Schumann, March 25, 1838.

My lame hand makes me wretched sometimes—here especially. It grows worse, too, as I don't mind admitting to you. I often bemoan my fate, and demand to know why Heaven should send me this particular trial.[19]

[19]. Letter to Clara Wieck, Vienna, December 3, 1838.

1846

But for favorable outside circumstances who knows what would have become of me, or whether I should have defeated the fate to which talent without means so often falls a prey.[20]

[20]. Letter to Ludwig Meinardus, Dresden, September 3, 1846.

Friends

1828

Whether we shall meet again, the fates alone can tell, but the world is not big enough, after all, to keep people apart, particularly real friends. Let us not bewail our losses, for fate has always sealed the mouths of men with her giant hand, though never their hearts.[21]

21. Letter to G. Rosen, August 14, 1828.

When we have to part from dear friends, and we are bidding them goodbye, our souls vibrate with a soft sad minor chord which is rarely heard. The twilight hours of our dead childhood, the pictures of the fleeting present, and the long vista of future years, all chime together like a peal of bells in one long drawn chord. The brilliant future strives to displace the gentle past, and vague tender feelings are having a mild contest in our hearts. And then comes that sweet angel of sadness, who would fain make us weep, but cannot, for he is smiling himself. Oh, for the lovely rainbow in the excited soul, when the sun of joy is shining, through heavenly tears are falling! Oh, for that sadness, when the heart is full to overflowing, and weeps and smiles, and weeps again![22]

22. Letter to his Mother, Leipzig, October 24, 1828.

1829

I have spent many a pure, beautiful hour with Rosen, and we have had those regular cozy winter chats, round the stove, in a warm comfortable room, which one misses in summer Semmel had by no means disturbed my friendship with Rosen, but still he had shared it, and my confidence had been divided, and so a silly, childish, youthful pride came between us, as so often happens among fellows who really like one another very much. I liked Semmel in quite a different way from Rosen. With Semmel my affection took a stronger, more manly and sensible form; with Rosen, I was more talkative, soft and impressionable, but both had equally frank and noble natures. Now, there are moments when one would rather only speak to one, even though one likes another fellow quite as well; and thus it happened that occasionally one of them felt aggrieved from a fancied want of confidence, because perhaps I had told one what I had forgotten to tell the other, or one of them would put a wrong construction on something I had said. Well, you can just imagine how it was.[23]

23. Letter to his Mother, Heidelberg, November 11, 1829.

1831

A long suppressed discord between two friends is much more cutting and dangerous than a frank outspoken reproach.[24]

24. Letter to his Mother, Leipzig, February 18, 1831.

Nature

1828

Nature best teaches how to pray, and how to reverence all the gifts the Almighty has given us. She is like a vast outspread handkerchief, embroidered with God's eternal name, on which we may dry alike the tears of sorrow and of joy; she turns weeping into ecstasy, and fills our hearts with speechless, quiet reverence and resignation.[25]

25. Letter to his Mother, Leipzig, August 3, 1828.

1829

Distance, which dulls the visual world, only renders the world of memory more distinct. Enthusiasm is changed to glowing classic calm and its expression is refined to a Goethe-like thoughtfulness.[26]

26. Reflections on the view of Rigi in Switzerland, in a letter to his Mother, Berne, August 31, 1829.

1833

How nice it is, when a sunbeam quivers over the piano, as though playing with sound, which, after all, is only sounding light.[27]

27. Letter to Clara Wieck, Leipzig, May 23, 1833.

Love

1828

I went to sleep very sorrowfully. Dreams hovered about me, until my good genius exclaimed:—'Your mother's birthday is near.' Then my visions took definite shape, and I dreamed that a world of hearts lay before me. Crushed and penitent souls flitted hither and thither, and those who had been saved and healed hovered round them and gently soothed their sorrows. Then, from the East there came a deep voice, clear and sweet as a bell, and the question thrilled through every heart:—'Whose love endures the longest?' Oh, how all the souls trembled at that sweet question! they crowded round, and each one said:—'Mine.' Aeolian harps accompanied the voices, and a blissful dawn rested on all the blossoms. And again the voice was heard:—'Whose love endures the longest?' and the hearts of Friendship came forward and said:—'A friend's love endures the longest, for it is unobtrusive and unconstrained.' But a wounded soul came flying from the West, and her murmured words sounded like a far away echo:—'Alas I was deceived in my friend's love, for it was very selfish.' Then all the souls quivered and shrank back before the question of that wounded soul. And the voice from the East rang out again: —'Whose love endures the longest?' And the hearts of Early Love appeared, and said: 'The lover's love endures the longest, for it is the most ardent of any .' But as they were declaring this so joyfully, and young hearts began once more to think of this beautiful world and the sunny spring time of first love, a down-trodden heart struggled out of the West, and sadly moaned:—'Not that love either, for my lover only caused me tears of grief, and then left me alone with my sorrows, and my young heart was withered.' And once more it flashed from the East, but there was sorrow and anger in the voice, as the great question again ran through the realm:— 'Is there no love which endures the longest?' And behold, a heart that had been lost, and saved again, spoke, and said: 'A mother's love endures the -longest, for she loves unselfishly.'[28]

1830

The truest love lies more in the spirit and in the imagination than in externals best way of learning to love is to be sent away for ten years among strangers; the result is a strong, undimmed affection.[29]

28. Letter to his Mother, Leipzig, November 25, 1828.

29. Letter to his Mother, Heidelberg, February 24, 1830.

Women

1829

Imagine the highest and loveliest type of womanhood, in the full pride of serene beauty, and a foaming panther, obedient to the touch of her light, triumphant fingers. Her steed, for all his restiveness, nuzzles her hand, and her head is proudly uplifted. Is it not a sublime picture of beauty's power to bind all things, even brute strength, with a spell?[30]

30. Letter to his Mother, Heidelberg, May 24, 1829, on seeing Dannecker's sculpture, 'Ariadne.'

Englishwomen love with their intellects—that is, they love a Brutus, a Lord Byron, a Mozart, or a Raphael, and are not so much attracted by the physical beauty of an Apollo or an Adonis, unless it enshrines a beautiful mind. Italian women do the exact opposite, and love with their hearts only. German women love with both heart and intellect as a rule, unless they fall in love with a circus-rider, a dancer, or some Croesus ready to marry them on the spot.[31]

1836

Feminine composers are so few that their names might be written on a rose leaf; and for this reason we keep watch for them, and do not allow any of their works to pass unnoticed. When a maiden neglects ribbons and flowers to write notes, she must have ten times more reasons for composing than we who only write in the hope of immortality.[32]

1838

We have followed Julie Baroni-Cavalcabo, who is a pupil of Mozart's son, with special interest till now; she possesses, next to Clara Wieck and Delphine Hill Handley, the richest musical vein among all her feminine contemporaries who have ventured into publicity; and, besides, a strong sense of proportion, form, and gradation, with qualities that must display themselves in her vocal compositions, much feeling, and melodious expression.[33]

I am one of the greatest admirers of beautiful women; I simply delight in them, and revel in praising your sex. So if ever we are walking together through the streets of Vienna, and meet somebody pretty, and I should exclaim, 'Oh, Clara, look at that divine creature,' or something of that sort, you must not be alarmed, or scold.[34]

Arts

1828

History, that eternally misinterpreted oracle, slumbers amidst beautiful ruins and tombs, and ruined Pompeii will ever be tearfully staring, empty and speechless, at petty mankind, just like a satire on the present time.[35]

---

31. Letter to his Sister-in-Law, Theresa Schumann, Brescia, September 16, 1829.

32. 'Capriccios and other short Studies,' in *Neue Zeitschrift für Musik*, 1836.

33. 'Fantasias, Capriccios, etc., for the Pianoforte,' in *Neue Zeitschrift für Musik*, 1838.

34. Letter to Clara Wieck, Leipzig, April 13, 1838.

35. Letter to William Götte, Schneeberg, October 2, 1828

1829

How dull our modern architecture is, with its symmetrical streets, two miles long, compared to a place like this (Rudesheim), where every turn brings something new and interesting![36]

36. Letter to his Mother, Heidelberg, May 24, 1829.

1833

The cultivated musician may study a Madonna by Raphael, the painter a symphony by Mozart, with equal advantage. Yet more: in the sculptor the actor's art becomes fixed, the actor transforms the sculptor's work into living forms, the painter turns a poem into a painting, the musician sets a picture to music.

......

The aesthetic principle is the same in every art; only the material differs.

......

Music—so different from painting is the art which we most enjoy when gathered together socially, and which is comprehended by a thousand at once, in one moment.

......

It is difficult to believe that music, the essentially romantic art, can form a distinctly romantic school within it.[37]

37. Schumann's Diary, 1833 or before.

1835

In no other art is demonstration so difficult as in music. Science fights with mathematics and logic; poetry wields the golden, decisive, spoken word; other arts have chosen Nature, whose forms they borrow, as their judge,—but music is an orphan, whose father and mother none can name; and perhaps in the mystery of her origin lies half her charm.[38]

38. 'Ferdinand Hiller,' in *Neue Zeitschrift für Musik*, 1835.

1847

Congratulations on the inauguration of your scheme [the founding of the Universal German Society of Musicians]. I think one[committee should consider 'the protection of classical music against modern adaptations.' Another committee should be formed for 'the research and restoration of corrupted passages in classical works.' A very great service, for instance, could be performed by looking into Mozart's *Requiem*, about which the greatest misconceptions are still current, for the existing version is not merely corrupt, but, except for certain numbers, spurious.

Next I should like to raise the question of 'the use of French for titles,' also 'the misuse of Italian for marks of expression,' by Germans in their own compositions. I should be glad if you would move 'the abolition of French titles,' and 'the rejection of such Italian expressions as may be rendered as well, if not better, in German.'[39]

39. Letter to Franz Brendel, Dresden, August 8, 1847.

Chapter Thirteen

Schumann's Reflections on his Life as a Student

1828
School days are over; the world lies before me. I could hardly keep back my tears as I came out of school for the last time, though I was really more glad than sorry. The time has come for me to show my mettle. Here I am, without guide, teacher, or father, flung helplessly into the darkness of life's unknown; and yet the world has never seemed fairer than at this moment, as I cheerfully face its storms. This is the time when a young man's soul glows with all things good and beautiful, and his ideals dwell with the gods of Greece in youth's bright Olympus.[1]

1. Letter to Emil Flechsig, Zwickau, March 17, 1828.

I arrived here last Thursday, quite well, though a little depressed, and took my position as a student and a citizen in this big, spacious city, in the stir of life and the great world. After my few days here I still feel quite well, though not quite happy. My whole heart cries out for the quieter home where I was born and spent such happy days with Nature. How shall I come into touch with Nature here? There is neither valley, mountain, nor wood, where I can indulge in meditation, no spot where I can be alone, except this shut-up room, overlooking the noisy street ...

I am perplexed beyond measure by the choice of a study. Chilly jurisprudence, with its ice-cold definitions, would crush the life out of me from the start. Medicine I will not, theology I cannot study. Thus I struggle endlessly with myself, and look in vain for some one to tell me what to do. And yet—there is no help for it; I must choose law. However cut and dried it may be, I will conquer, and where there's a will there's a way ...

As to my state of mind, it is neither worse nor better than before. I go regularly to lectures, practice two hours a day, read a few hours, or go for a walk—my sole recreation. At Zweinaundorf, a village lying in the loveliest part of the country round here, I often spend whole days alone, working, writing poetry, and so on. I have not cultivated the acquaintance of a single student so far. I go to the fencing-school, am sociable, and behave decently in every way, but am extremely cautious about becoming intimate with anyone. I find that, without being stand-offish, I can make these fellows keep their distance and not treat one as a freshman in the corps.[2]

My life at Leipzig creeps on in the old, wretched, everyday track, and I would sooner be at Jericho than here. The portraits of my father, of Jean Paul, and of Napoleon, hang over my desk in gold frames, and the bookcase looks splendid. I go to lecture as regular as clockwork, play the piano a great deal, and often read; play a game of chess every evening with Flechsig, and go for a two or three hours' walk. l have fencing-school, because it is absolutely necessary, and even useful. But I never have been a fighting character, and never shall be, and you need to be alarmed about duels.[3]

The rest of my life is most insipid and monotonous, and creeps comfortably along at a snail's pace. I frequently go for a walk all by myself, play the piano a great deal, often go to lectures, etc. I rarely if ever go to the tavern, etc., but fence a little … and that is the whole of my college life.[4]

1829

I am in excellent spirits, really happy by moments, and am working well and steadily. Thibaut and Mittermayer have given me a taste for law. I begin to realize its true value in furthering the highest interests of mankind. But oh!, the difference between that Leipzig automaton, with one eye on a regular professorship, reading out his dull paragraphs phlegmatically, and Thibaut here, who, though twice his age, overflows with vivacity and intelligence, and can hardly find time or words to express all his ideas.

2. Letter to his Mother, Leipzig, May 21, 1828.

3. Letter to his Mother, Leipzig, June 29, 1828.

4. Letter to his Mother, Leipzig, August 22, 1828.

The Heidelberg student is much misrepresented. He is very quiet, rather apt to stand upon ceremony and affect fine manners, because he is not yet sure of himself. A young man of any grit develops best under a system of repression, and this perpetual lounging with no one but students limits his mental outlook, and injures him incalculably for practical life. Heidelberg has always this advantage, that its fine scenery does much to distract students from dissipation and drinking. They are far steadier here than at Leipzig. I have not found my way into any families yet. Time enough for that in the winter, when I shall no doubt be glad to go out a good deal, as there are plenty of girls here to make love to! You meet dozens of students engaged—with the consent of the parents. The girls naturally lose their sentimental hearts to the only men they see, and, as they meet no one but students, engagements among them are the order of the day. But have no fear for me.[5]

5. Letter to his Mother, Heidelberg, July 17, 1829.

To one of your questions I must give a mournful answer—I mean about my music and piano playing. Alas! mother, it is almost quite at an end; I play but rarely now, and very badly. The grand Genius of Music is gently extinguishing his torch, and all that I have ever done in music seems like a beautiful dream which I can hardly believe has ever existed. And yet, believe me, *if ever I could have done any good in the world it would have been in music*, and I feel sure (without at all overrating my capabilities) that I have got creative power. But earning one's bread is another thing! Studying law has frozen and dried me up to such an extent that no flower of my imagination could possibly come into bloom.[6]

6. Letter to his Mother, Heidelberg, November 11, 1829.

1830

[At a concert] I played Moscheles's 'Alexander' Variations. There was absolutely no end to the 'bravos' and 'encores,' and I really felt quite hot and uncomfortable. course I had been practicing the piece for eight weeks, and felt that I was playing really well.

Sad to say, I am out somewhere almost every evening, either at balls, or evening parties, etc. Fridays I am always at Thibaut's, Tuesdays at Mittermayer's, Thursdays in a select set of angelic Englishwomen, Mondays in the Musik-verein, Saturdays with the Grand Duchess … [7]

7. Letter to Julius Schumann, Heidelberg, February 11, 1830.

The chief reason against my staying longer at Heidelberg is the everlasting sickening cry of money, as it would cost just as much again. And yet I do not know: I am in my first youth, am not so very poor, can look forward here to many intellectual enjoyments, have charming acquaintances, and good men for my friends, so why should I destroy the happy present, and the bright future, for the sake of 200 florins?

Now for something very unpalatable—my money matters. They are in a bad way, and, by Jove, I am in debt! I wish I could show you the tailor's and bootmaker's bills alone. The tailor has had 90 florin out of me since Easter, and I still owe him 55 florin. My cloak was 85 florin, two pairs of black trousers 36 florin. I have further had my blue cloth dress coat and black coat turned, and was obliged to get a traveling suit, not to mention other repairs. At the bootmaker's the outlook is not much brighter. A pair of mountain boots came on the top of sundry other pairs, and a new pair of shoes followed quickly in the rear of various repairs and re-solings, so that the result is perfectly appalling. Then I must eat and drink; and I play the piano, and smoke, and sometimes, but not often, drive to Mannheim. I also require money for lectures, and want books and music, all of which costs a terrible lot of money. Those confounded fancy balls, tipping various people, subscriptions to the museum, and cigars—oh, those cigars!—the piano tuner, the laundress, the shoe-black, candles, soap, all my dear friends who expect a wretched glass of beer, the man at the museum who brings me the newspapers! I should absolutely despair, if I were not on the verge of desperation already! For four weary weeks I have not had a penny in my pocket; and there is no lack of mysterious hints, letters, and reproachful looks as I walk about the streets.[8]

8. Letter to his Mother, Heidelberg, February 24, 1830

It is certainly very jolly here; but there are, alas, such things as Debts. This summer life is glorious. I get up every morning at four, when the sky is the tenderest blue, and study Pandicts, etc., till eight. From eight to ten I play the piano; from ten to twelve there is a lecture by Thibaut or Mittermayer. From twelve to two I stroll about the town, and have my dinner. From two to four I go and see Zacharia and Johannsen, and then I am off to the castle, or down to the Rhine, or away to my beloved hills. This is usually the order of my day. Remember that if I had gone on study ing in Leipzig, I should have claimed your hospitality for a week last Michaelmas, Christmas, and Easter, and that my breakfasts, wine, cigars, champagne, and billiards would have mounted up very considerably. Seriously, remember that yesterday my thrice-renewed bill for 150 florin was due to a college money lender, and that I must procure the money by June 18th. Remember that the lectures cost me 50 florin this half, and that I am being specially coached by Professor Johannsen, which alone costs me 80 florin. Remember, I implore of you, that since last winter I have been taking lessons in French, Italian, English, and Spanish.[9]

9. Letter to Carl Schumann, Heidelberg, June 3, 1830.

My own simple idyll is compounded of music, jurisprudence, and poetry; poetry is to the prose of life as the shining gold setting to the hard, glittering diamond. I get up early, work from four to seven, sit at the piano from seven to nine, and am then off to Thibaut. The afternoon is divided between lectures and lessons or reading in English and Italian; the evening I spend with friends or out-of-doors. There you have the whole truth. I feel sometimes that I am not a practical person, but Providence alone is responsible for that, since it endowed me with imagination to unravel and illuminate the tangled problems of the future. You may be sure I should like to be great in my profession, and I am really not wanting in goodwill and energy My failure to rise above the average will be no fault of mine, but of circumstances; perhaps, also, of my own heart, to which Latin has always been quite alien. Chance alone, or some heaven-sent turn of fortune, may lift the dark curtain which veils my future. Thibaut, for instance, does not encourage me to pursue my law studies, because, as he says, I was 'not born a bureaucrat,' and real efficiency is unattainable without native inclination. No automatic, machine-made lawyer, therefore, can excel in his profession. I cannot withhold from you these, my real convictions.[10]

10. Letter to his Mother, Heidelberg, July 1, 1830.

My life has been for twenty years one long struggle between poetry and prose, or, let us say, music and law. My aims were as high in practical life as in art. I hoped to find scope for my energies and my powers of overcoming difficulties in a wide sphere of work. But what prospects are there, particularly in Saxony, for an ordinary plebeian, who has neither interest nor fortune, nor any real love for pettifogging legal details? At Leipzig I never troubled myself about my career, but dreamed and pottered away my time without any tangible results. Here I have worked better, but my stay in both places has only tended to strengthen my leaning towards art. Now I stand at the crossroads, trembling before the question, Whither? My own instinct points to art, and I believe it to be the right road, but it has always seemed to me—you will not be hurt if I whisper it lovingly—that you rather barred my way in that direction. I quite see your excellent motherly reasons, known to both of us as 'a precarious future' and 'an uncertain livelihood.'

But let us look a little further. A man can know no greater torment than to look forward to an unhappy, empty, and lifeless future of his own planning; but neither is it easy for him to choose a profession directly opposed to that for which he was destined from his youth. Such a change means patience, confidence, and a rapid training. My fancy is young, and sheds its halo over the artist-life; I have also arrived at the certainty that, given a good teacher and six years' steady, hard work, I shall be able to hold my own against any pianist, for pianoforte playing is merely a matter of mechanical perfection. I have, besides, an occasional flight of imagination, and what is perhaps a real inspiration to compose.

This brings me to the question—which shall I choose? I can only make my mark in one or the other. I tell myself that if I give my whole mind to a thing I am bound to succeed, dear Mother, in the end, through steady application. Thus battle within rages more fiercely than ever. Sometimes I am foolhearty, and confident in my own tenacity; at others, doubtful, when I think of the immense stretch of road before me which I might by this time have covered. As for Thibaut, he has long been advising me to take up music. I should be very glad if you would write to him, and I know he would be pleased.

If I keep to law it certainly means spending another winter here to attend Thibaut's lectures on the Pandects, which no law student can afford to miss. If I decide on music, I must as certainly leave here and return to Leipzig. I should be quite glad to go under Wieck, who knows me, and can gauge my capabilities. Later on I should want a year in Vienna, and, if possible, lessons from Moscheles. And now, dear Mother, one request which you will perhaps be glad to fulfill.

Will you write yourself to Wieck at Leipzig, and ask him plainly what he thinks of me and my scheme? Please let me have a speedy reply, telling me your decision, so that I can hasten my departure from Heidelberg, loath as I am to leave this paradise, my many friends, and my bright dreams. Enclose this letter in your own to Wieck, if you like. In any case the matter must be settled by Michaelmas; then I will work, vigorously and without regrets, at my chosen profession.[11]

11. Letter to his Mother, Heidelberg, July 30, 1830.

It has taken a long time for the tumult of my ideas to quiet down. What an upheaval the reading of those two letters caused! I am just beginning to feel more collected. I at once took courage on reading your letter, and concluded that Atlas was overthrown. In his place stood a child of the Sun, pointing to the east, saying, 'Beware of thwarting Nature, lest thy good genius take his flight forever. The road to science lies over ice-clad mountains; the road to art also lies over mountains, but they are tropical, set with flowers, hopes, and dreams.' Such was the state of my feelings on first reading your letter and my mother's, but I am much calmer now. I choose art, and by this decision I will, can, and must abide. I can bid good-bye without a tear to a science which I do not love and barely respect; but it is not without qualms that I look down the long vista leading to the goal I have set myself. I assure you I am modest, as, indeed, I have reason to be; but I am also courageous, patient, trusting, and teachable. I put myself in your hands with entire confidence. Take me as I am, and be patient with me in everything. Reproaches shall not depress me, nor praise make me idle. A few bucketfuls of cold, real cold, theory will not hurt me and I shall not dodge the wetting. Take my hand and lead me, honored Master, for I will follow you blindly; and never shift the bandage from my eyes, lest they be dazzled by the splendor. If I could show you my inner self at this moment, you would see me at peace in a world bathed with the fragrance of the dawn.[12]

12. Letter to Friedrich Wieck, Heidelberg, August 21, 1830.

The signpost pointing toward Art says: 'If you are diligent you can reach your goal in three years.' Law says: 'In three years you may, perhaps, be an accessist earning sixteen groschen a year. Art continues: 'I am free as air, and the whole world is my haven.' Law says with a shrug: 'My practice involves constant subordination at every step of the way, and immaculate dress.' Art goes on to say: 'Where I am, there is beauty; I rule the heart, whose emotions I have called into being; I am unshackled and infinite; I compose and am immortal,' etc. Law says sternly: 'I have nothing to offer but musty deeds, village squabbles, or, with exceptional luck, the exciting mystery of a sudden death.' I will not turn the conversation on to baser considerations, such as the comparative lucrativeness of the two professions, since the answer is self-evident.[13]

13. Letter to his Mother, Heidelberg, August 22, 1830.

You say you were incapable of praying after you had read my letter, telling you of my decision. Can that be really true? I shall not be much satisfaction to you as I am, but I vow that if I stuck to law I should shoot myself from sheer boredom when I became a junior barrister.[14]

14. Letter to his Mother, Leipzig, November 15, 1830.

1831

By Jove, it is quite true, when I tell you that for the last fortnight I have only eaten meat about twice, and lived upon plain potatoes. I am too shy to go to Barth, and, after all, ten or twenty thalers would not help me much, as I owe both Luhe and my board keeper (who is most rude to me, because I have not paid him for three months) from sixty to seventy thalers, not to mention my debt to Wieck! I have also had to pawn your watch, and one book after the other finds its way to the second-hand booksellers. You may imagine how much I am losing. The day before yesterday I went in despair to Wieck, and borrowed a thaler.[15]

15. Letter to his Mother, Leipzig, February 21, 1831.

I just keep jogging on. It is the fault of all vivid young minds that they aspire to too much at once; it only makes their work more complicated, and their spirit more restless. But quiet old age will calm down and level all that. I can only have four aims to choose from conducting, teaching, playing, and composing. Hummel combines all four, but in my case it will probably be one of the last two. If only I could do one thing well, instead of many things badly, as I have always done! Still, the principal thing for me to keep in view, is to lead a pure, steady, sober life. If I stick to that, my guardian angel will not desert me; he now sometimes almost possesses me for a little while.[16]

16. Letter to his Mother, Leipzig, May 31, 1831.

Chapter Fourteen

Schumann's Reflections on his Daily Routine

1829

I have left my swell, aristocratic lodgings, and taken up my abode in a very cozy little 'poet's den,' which strikingly resembles my old green room at Zwickau. I need not tell you how infinitely more comfortable I am here, and how often I imagine myself at Zwickau, that dear little home, containing my earliest recollections, where I wrote my first verses, smoked my first cigar, developed my earliest theories, where, in short, the boy quietly and unconsciously grew into a man.

As to my life here, I am industrious and regular; but am trying to spend as little as possible, and only allow myself a very frugal meal (for Heidelberg, I mean), soup, boiled beef, joint, and dessert, and so manage to save 18 kreutzer a day. The principal reason of my doing this was to enable me to take French lessons, which are ruinously expensive here, and cost 8 groschen the hour. But I shall not rest until I can read and speak French just as well as German, for I see more and more how necessary it is, and often think sadly how my dear father was always telling me so. The lectures for this half will cost me 70 fl., entrance fee to museum 14 fl., piano hire 40 fl., rent of rooms 45 fl., French lessons 36 fl., total 215 fl. or 130 thalers. Now I have not put down either food or drink, tailor or bootmaker, and not a single book. Can I exist on that sum? Heavens! How well I can understand all that Christ endured![1]

1. Letter to his Mother, Heidelberg, November 11, 1829.

1831

I have left my cold bare rooms at N's, with their shabby-genteel air, and have taken up my abode near the river. So now, from my front room I see a beautiful green garden with red houses peeping in, and have a view of the whole Eastern sky, and can see the sun rise, which I enjoy like a child every morning over my coffee. But my back room is far nicer; there is something so warm and cosy about it. I look out on bright gardens, and a clacking millwheel with a wide rushing stream, while in the evening I see the moon rise and get the most glorious sunsets.[2]

2. Letter to his Mother, Leipzig, October 14, 1831.

1832

I feel very well; I am very industrious, and have almost quite given up smoking cigars and drinking beer.[3]

3. Letter to his family, Leipzig, April 28, 1832.

I spring out of bed, nimble as a deer, at about five o'clock, and devote myself to my accounts, my diary and my correspondence. Then I work, compose or read a little by turns, up to eleven. Then comes dinner, after which I read a little French or a newspaper. From three to six I generally take a solitary walk, usually the road to Connewitz.[4]

4. Letter to his Mother, Leipzig, May 8, 1832.

1834

I live quite simply. I have given up drinking any spirits, and walk a great deal every day with my good friend Ludwig Schunke. I have also worked better than for weeks past.

You ask if I have enough money. I must confess—no. But, believe me, these cares are inconsiderable compared with life's sufferings. Were they healed, happiness and energy would return and soon disperse the lighter troubles.[5]

5. Letter to his Mother, Leipzig, January 4, 1834.

I have regained my old nerve in improvising before people, and performed at Barth's the other day, where I went to dinner.[6]

6. Letter to his Mother, Leipzig, March 19, 1834.

1836

With my usual liking for the extraordinary, I am now one of the slightest smokers and 'Bavarians,' though I was once the most hardened offender. Four cigars a day, and for the last two months no beer at all. As a result everything goes like clockwork, and I am really proud of myself.[7]

7. Letter to his Sister-in-Law, Theresa Schumann, Leipzig, April 1, 1836.

1838

I rise early, usually before six, and this first hour is the most precious of my whole day.[8]

8. Letter to Clara Wieck, Leipzig, March 17–19, 1838.

I give several hours daily to the study of Bach and Beethoven, outside my own studies. I carry on a large and often complicated correspondence methodically. I stay quietly at home in Saxony, in spite of my twenty-eight years and my quick-stirring artist's pulse. I save money, and spend nothing on feasting or betting, but take my peaceful walk to Gohlis, as of old, for sole recreation.[9]

9. Letter to Clara Wieck, Leipzig, May 10, 1838.

1854

I am at present occupied with the ancients, Homer and the Greeks. In Plato especially I have found some splendid passages.[10]

10. Letter to Joachim, Düsseldorf, February 6, 1854.

I also feel the need for manuscript paper, as I sometimes feel inclined to write a little music. My life here is very simple. I take my chief pleasure in the view of Bonn ... I should like to know too, dear Clara, whether you have by chance sent me clothes or cigars?[11]

11. Letter to Clara Schumann, Endenich, September 14, 1854.

I have just returned from Bonn, where I paid my customary visit to Beethoven's statue, which always delights me.[12]

12. Letter to Clara Schumann, Endenich, September 18, 1854.

Chapter Fifteen

Schumann's Descriptions of his Wife, Clara

1832

You are to me, my dear Clara, not a sister or a girl friend, but the pilgrim's distant shrine.[1]

1. Letter to Clara Wieck, Leipzig, January 11, 1832.

1833

I ask—what sustains this continual interest in her?. Is it the 'wonder child' herself, at whose stretches of tenths people shake their heads, while they are amazed at them? Or the most difficult difficulties which she sportively flings towards the public like flower garlands?

......

I know not; I only feel that here we are subdued by genius, which men still hold in respect. In short, we here divine the presence of a power of which much is spoken, while few indeed possess it.

......

To Clara we dare no longer apply the measuring scale of age, but only that of fulfillment.

......

Clara Wieck is the first German artist.[2]

2. Schumann's Diary, 1833 or before.

Clara, who is as fond of me as ever, is the same wild and fanciful little person, skipping and tearing about like a child one moment, and full of serious sayings the next. It is a pleasure to watch the increasing rapidity with which she unfolds the treasures of her heart and mind, as a flower unfolds its petals.[3]

3. Letter to his Mother, Leipzig, June 28, 1833.

I might also express a hope that the union of our names on the title-page may be symbolic of a union of our thoughts and ideas in the future. This is all a poor beggar like myself can do.[4]

4. Letter to Clara Wieck, Leipzig, August 2, 1833.

1837

We must remember that, as an artist, she already stands on the topmost peak of our time, at a height where nothing is hidden from her. Of those deeps where Sebastian Bach has penetrated so profoundly that even the miner's lamp threatens to become extinguished in their darkness, of those clouds which Beethoven grasped with his Titantic fist, all that our modern day has united of these heights and depths, the young artist knows, and tells of them with charming maidenly wisdom; yet with all this she has raised expectation regarding herself to such a height, that one is troubled when one considers what it must all lead to. I will not venture to predict. [5]

5. 'Museum,' in *Neue Zeitschrift für Musik*, 1837.

My feeling towards Clara, which thrills in every fibre of my being, is no passing desire, no violent emotion, no surface thing, but the deep rooted conviction that everything augurs well for the happiness of our union.[6]

6. Letter to Friedrich Wieck, September 13, 1837.

Oh, Clara, how sad it is that we are doomed to spend our best years apart. Wherever I go I hear nothing but praises of your beautiful self. I alone am debarred from talking to you, listening to you, while you have to exist on a few precious memories. You are passionate and reasonable, suspicious and trustful, loving and angry, by turns.[7]

7. Letter to Clara Wieck, November 29, 1837.

I never leave you, but follow everywhere, though unseen. The figure fades away, but love and faith are unchanging …

Sit down beside me now, slip your arm round me, and let us gaze peacefully, blissfully, into each other's eyes. This world holds two lovers. It is just striking the third quarter. They are singing a chorale in the distance. Tell me, do you know those two lovers? How happy we are, Clara! Let us kneel together, Clara, my Clara, so close that I can touch you, in this solemn hour.

My dear one, then, I have wept for joy to think that you are mine, and often wonder if I deserve you. One would think that no one man's heart and brain could stand all the things that are crowded into one day. Where do these thousands of thoughts, wishes, sorrows, joys, and hopes, come from? Day in, day out, the procession goes on. But how light-hearted I was yesterday and the day before! There shone out of your letters so noble a spirit, such faith, such a wealth of love! What would I not do for love of you, my own Clara! The knights of old were better off; they could go through fire or slay dragons to win their ladies, but we of today have to content ourselves with more prosaic methods, such as smoking fewer cigars, and the like. There are terrible hours when your image forsakes me, when I wonder anxiously whether I have ordered my life as wisely as I might, whether I had any right to bind you to me ...

Accustomed to easy victory over difficulties, to the smiles of fortune, and to affection, I have been spoiled by having things made too easy for me, and now I have to face refusal, insult, and calumny. Upon my word, I have no cause to do anything to please your father. Has he not ceased to show the smallest interest in me this long time past? Has he not hunted out and displayed all my failings to lower me in your estimation, and refused to recognize in me the qualities which he himself lacks? I will not cringe or give way to him one inch, neither will I beg for you at his hands A certain letter of his to me contains expressions which I should hesitate about forgiving, should the Almighty Himself ask it of me. I was silent that once, remembering that he was your father; but the humiliation of it! I bore it once, but I could not do it again, even should it mean losing you. I assure you my disposition is towards gentleness and goodness, and my heart is still pure as it left the Creator's hands; but there is a limit to my patience, and I may yet show my claws ...

Don't play quite so well, do you hear? Their enthusiasm must be kept within bounds, for with every storm of applause your father pushes me a little farther from you, remember.[8]

8. Letter to Clara Wieck, Leipzig, December 22, 1837 through January 5, 1838.

1838

All the papers are full of you, as I expected. I go to the museum every day and read the Vienna notices. You say I do not realize what you are as an artist, and you are partly right, partly quite wrong. You may have strengthened your individuality, reached a higher stage of perfection, but I know my dear enthusiastic girl so well of old that I could tell her playing miles away.

A girl like you might well tempt one to sin against his conscience. But you would restore him to virtue by your own, my Clara—that virtue which has brought me back to life, and is a perpetual inspiration to greater purity. I was a poor, beaten wretch, who for eighteen months could neither pray nor weep, for eye and heart were cold and hard as iron. And now, what a change! Your love and loyalty have made me a new creature. I sometimes feel as if my heart were crossed by a thousand narrow intersecting paths, along which my thoughts and feeling race up and down, and in and out, like human beings, asking, Whither does this way lead? and that? and all the ways? And the answer is always the same: 'to Clara.'

Will you not pay a visit to our beloved Schubert and Beethoven? Take with you some sprigs of myrtle, twine them together in twos, and lay them on the graves, if you can. Whisper your name and mine as you do it—not a word besides.[9]

How shall I begin to tell you what a different creature you are making of me, you dear, splendid person! Sometimes as I go through your letters I feel like the first man, as he was led by an angel through the whole new creation; as they go from height to height, where each new prospect is fairer than the last, the angel says: 'All this is thine.' If I once said I only loved you because of your goodness, it was only half true. Everything is so harmoniously combined in your nature that I cannot think of you apart from your music—and so I love the one with the other.[10]

[You are] the most glorious of girls, from whom I cannot be parted, who is also the greatest of artists. I will say no more of my happiness in possessing a girl with whom I have grown to be one through art, intellectual affinities, the regular intercourse of years, and the deepest and holiest affection.[11]

Her whole nature is made up of love and devotion and gratitude. She makes me very happy in the midst of this material Viennese life.[12]

My strength always fails me when I am left long without a sign from you. Depression sets in, and I feel as if I were being swathed in endless black fabrics and garmets, and stowed away an indescribable sensation.[13]

9. Letter to Clara Wieck, Leipzig, February 6, 1838.

10. Letter to Clara Wieck, Leipzig, March 17–19, 1838.

11. Letter to Edward and Karl Schumann, Leipzig, March 19, 1838.

12. Letter to Theresa Schumann, Vienna, December 18, 1838.

13. Letter to Clara Wieck, Vienna, December 18, 1838.

1839

I confess I was ready to put an end to myself with all possible speed a few days ago, but I decided to wait for your next letters.[14]

Fate has ordained that we should fight our way step by step; but when, one day, we stand at the alter, our 'yes' will be spoken with a conviction, an assured faith in our future happiness, that is quite without parallel.

One thing I know, my gentle personality made an impression on you when you were very young. I think you would have been different but for knowing me. You will leave me this comforting assurance? I taught you to love, your father to hate—in the best sense of the word, for there are good haters. Under my influence you grew to be the ideal partner of my joys and sorrows. You were my best pupil, and have rewarded me by giving me yourself.[15]

1840

No one can touch you, for your playing comes from your heart.[16]

Clara is like me in this, much as she delights in, and actually needs, encouragement. She is indeed subject to fits of depression, which are quite inexplicable to me. Slender as she is, she is very healthy, and has the endurance of a man.[17]

14. Letter to Clara Wieck, Leipzig, May 18, 1839.

15. Letter to Clara Wieck, Leipzig, June 3, 1839.

16. Letter to Clara Wieck, Leipzig, March 20, 1840.

17. Letter to Gustav Keferstein, Leipzig, August 24, 1840.

140 Schumann: A Self-Portrait

1845

For her untiring zeal and energy in her art she really deserves everyone's love and encouragement; then, as a woman, she is indeed a gift from Heaven.[18]

18. Letter to Mendelssohn, Dresden, October 22, 1845.

Chapter Sixteen

Schumann on the Founding of the Neue Zeitschrift für Musik

1833

I have taken my own little band of congenial spirits, mostly music Students ... We are principally concerned with a plan for bringing out a new musical paper, which Hofmeister is to publish. Prospectuses and notices will be out next month. The whole thing is to be fresher and more varied in tone than the existing papers, and we aim at avoiding the conventional routine at all costs.[1]

Wieck has probably told you of the advent of a new musical periodical, which is to champion the cause of poetry by relentlessly attacking her present detractors. I need not, of course, impress upon you how much depends on the first numbers, which, without promising too much, ought to make the public realize that a perceptible gap has been filled.[2]

1834

Just now I have to devote my whole energy to the paper. The others are not to be depended on. Wieck is constantly on tour; Knorrill; Schunke has not much idea of wielding the pen; and who is left? Yet the paper is so extraordinarily successful that I go on working hard, but with satisfaction.[3]

1835

I am now the sole editor and proprietor. In the last quarter of last year there was not enough solid opinion and finished criticism. But there are to be many improvements now.[4]

---

1. Letter to his Mother, Leipzig, June 28, 1833.

2. Letter to Franz Otto, Leipzig, August 9, 1833.

3. Letter to his Mother, Leipzig, July 2, 1834.

4. Letter to Dr. Topken, Leipzig, February 6, 1835.

About the author

David Whitwell is a graduate ('with distinction') of the University of Michigan and the Catholic University of America, Washington D.C. (Ph.D., Musicology, Distinguished Alumni Award, 2000) and has studied conducting with Eugene Ormandy and at the Akademie für Musik, Vienna. Prior to coming to Northridge, Dr. Whitwell participated in concerts throughout the United States and Asia as Associate First Horn in the USAF Band and Orchestra in Washington, D.C., and in recitals throughout South America in cooperation with the United States State Department.

At the California State University, Northridge, which is in Los Angeles, Dr. Whitwell developed the CSUN Wind Ensemble into an ensemble of international reputation, with international tours to Europe in 1981 and 1989 and to Japan in 1984. The CSUN Wind Ensemble has made professional studio recordings for BBC (London), the Köln Westdeutscher Rundfunk (Germany), NOS National Radio (The Netherlands), Zürich Radio (Switzerland), the Television Broadcasting System (Japan) as well as for the United States State Department for broadcast on its 'Voice of America' program. The CSUN Wind Ensemble's recording with the Mirecourt Trio in 1982 was named the 'Record of the Year' by The Village Voice. Composers who have guest conducted Whitwell's ensembles include Aaron Copland, Ernest Krenek, Alan Hovhaness, Morton Gould, Karel Husa, Frank Erickson and Vaclav Nelhybel.

Dr. Whitwell has been a guest professor in 100 different universities and conservatories throughout the United States and in 23 foreign countries (most recently in China, in an elite school housed in the Forbidden City). Guest conducting experiences have included the Philadelphia Orchestra, Seattle Symphony Orchestra, the Czech Radio Orchestras of Brno and Bratislava, The National Youth Orchestra of Israel, as well as resident wind ensembles in Russia, Israel, Austria, Switzerland, Germany, England, Wales, The Netherlands, Portugal, Peru, Korea, Japan, Taiwan, Canada and the United States.

He is a past president of the College Band Directors National Association, a member of the Prasidium of the International Society for the Promotion of Band Music, and was a member of the founding board of directors of the World Association for Symphonic Bands and Ensembles (WASBE). In 1964 he was made an honorary life member of Kappa Kappa Psi, a national professional music fraternity. In September, 2001, he was a delegate to the UNESCO Conference on Global Music in Tokyo. He has been knighted by sovereign organizations in France, Portugal and Scotland and has been awarded the gold medal of Kerkrade, The Netherlands, and the silver medal of Wangen,

Germany, the highest honor given wind conductors in the United States, the medal of the Academy of Wind and Percussion Arts (National Band Association) and the highest honor given wind conductors in Austria, the gold medal of the Austrian Band Association. He is a member of the Hall of Fame of the California Music Educators Association.

Dr. Whitwell's publications include more than 127 articles on wind literature including publications in Music and Letters (London), the London Musical Times, the Mozart-Jahrbuch (Salzburg), and 39 books, among which is his 13-volume History and Literature of the Wind Band Ensemble and an 8-volume series on Aesthetics in Music. In addition to numerous modern editions of early wind band music his original compositions include 5 symphonies.

David Whitwell was named as one of six men who have determined the course of American bands during the second half of the 20th century, in the definitive history, The Twentieth Century American Wind Band (Meredith Music).

A doctoral dissertation by German Gonzales (2007, Arizona State University) is dedicated to the life and conducting career of David Whitwell through the year 1977. David Whitwell is one of nine men described by Paula A. Crider in The Conductor's Legacy (Chicago: GIA, 2010) as 'the legendary conductors' of the 20th century.

'I can't imagine the 2nd half of the 20th century—without David Whitwell and what he has given to all of the rest of us.' Frederick Fennell (1993)

www.ingramcontent.com/pod-product-compliance
Lightning Source LLC
Chambersburg PA
CBHW080451170426
43196CB00016B/2766